PRACTICAL STRATEGIES

FOR CRITICAL THINKING

PRACTICAL STRATEGIES

FOR CRITICAL THINKING

JAN REHNER
York University

HOUGHTON MIFFLIN COMPANY Boston Toronto
Geneva, Illinois Palo Alto Princeton, New Jersey

To Arthur

Sponsoring Editor: Kristin Watts Peri
Managing Development Editor: Melody Davies
Project Editor: Susan Westendorf
Production/Design Coordinator: Jennifer Waddell
Senior Manufacturing Coordinator: Marie Barnes
Marketing Manager: George Kane

Acknowledgments:

Part 1   From *The New Girl Friend and Other Stories* by Ruth
Rendell. Copyright © 1985 by Kinsmarkham Enterprises Ltd.
Reprinted by permission of Pantheon Books, a Division of
Random House, Inc.   *(continued on p. 175)*

Printed in U.S.A.

Library of Congress Catalog Card Number: 93-78679
ISBN: 0-395-67340-2

123456789–AM–97 96 95 94 93

CONTENTS

3 CRITICAL WRITING

PREFACE

This brief guide demystifies the process of critical thinking by identifying and illustrating a number of specific problem-solving strategies that students can apply to their own college courses. It encourages students to become more aware of their own patterns of thinking and to develop strategies for applying critical thinking systematically and creatively to the world around them. Throughout, the guiding questions are, "How does this strategy work?" and "How can I use this strategy to become a more effective critical reader, thinker, and writer?"

Critical thinking typically involves both a set of activities and a particular attitude toward thinking and learning. The practical activities of a critical thinker include, for example, various strategies for asking questions, testing assumptions, and generating ideas. One aim of this book is to make such activities explicit to students by providing a repertoire of strategies that can be applied to individual learning situations. The notion of application is central to the attitude of critical thinkers, who take an active rather than a passive approach to learning. Thus, a second aim is to encourage students to try the strategies in other courses and classrooms, in contexts that are personally meaningful or rooted in a particular academic discipline.

Practical Strategies for Critical Thinking can be used as a core text for critical skills and composition courses or in conjunction with a wide range of courses in the humanities and social sciences. The question, "How can I use this strategy to become a more effective critical reader, thinker, and writer?" is answered by linking each strategy to a particular critical skill. For instance, students can use *branching* as a strategy for generating ideas, *role-playing* for examining an issue from multiple perspectives, and *freewriting* for analyzing a text. In this way, students learn to recognize the kinds of problems and tasks that recur in a range of courses and begin to develop the thinking skills necessary to solve the problems and succeed in the tasks.

Moreover, in each of the three sections—on reading, thinking, and writing—the practical question, "How does this strategy work?" is answered by applying the strategy to the readings included in the text. Although these readings, both fiction and nonfiction, are entertaining and informative in themselves, the focus in each section is on the strategy and on modeling how the strategy works. For example, various strategies for raising questions are not merely listed, but also applied to specific readings. Consequently, students can easily trace how the strategies function. In fact, implicit in every section is the expectation that students will begin practicing strategies by applying them to new readings and assignments and by discovering for themselves how to set and solve problems.

Finally, although students can use *Practical Strategies for Critical Thinking* independently, the book assumes a community of learning, where dialogue and diverse voices animate the classrooms. The skill of critical thinking develops more quickly when both students and instructors engage spiritedly in the learning process and are willing to experiment and take risks. All the strategies presented have been tested in the classroom, and they are meant to be adaptable—to different kinds of courses, different academic disciplines, even to different kinds of students. Modifying them to suit particular needs is one of the pleasures inherent in using them.

I would like to thank the following reviewers for their insights and suggestions: Patsy Callaghan, Central Washington University; Anne C. Coon, Rochester Institute of Technology; Irene Gale, Kansas State University; and Don Tighe, Valencia Community College. I would also like to acknowledge the creative teaching and thinking of my own learning community, especially of my colleagues in the Faculty of Arts Centre for Academic Writing and the Critical Skills College Tutorial Programme at York University. In particular, Tom Greenwald, Joan Page, and John Spencer have shared with me many of their insights about teaching critical skills and, in so doing, have been my best teachers. Dianne Fair, a gifted educator of young children, has helped to remind me of what students of all ages need and want to learn. Special thanks are owed to Arthur Haberman, a steadfast and incisive critic who continues to give me his excellent advice. I would also like to thank Ric Kitowski and the editorial staff at Houghton Mifflin Company, particularly Kristin Watts Peri. Finally, I am most grateful to the many committed and energetic students whose questions over the years helped me learn how to write this book.

INTRODUCTION

Many people believe that, by the time they reach college, they should already be expert readers, thinkers, and writers. However, no matter how solid is your base of learning skills, college should and will present new challenges that require you to develop increasingly sophisticated levels of thinking. In addition, it will be necessary to learn how to adapt your reading, thinking, and writing skills to particular academic disciplines or fields of study. As you progress through college, you will notice that your courses in business, for example, will ask different questions, pose different problems, and require different kinds of writing than your courses on popular culture or English composition or European history. For these reasons, it is much more productive for you to think about the skills you have and the skills you will need as developmental. No one arrives at college already in possession of all the necessary skills; and few leave college without having developed their skills to read, think, and write critically.

Critical thinking is a term used to describe both a set of activities and a particular frame of mind or set of attitudes. Although thinking is invisible—you can see the results of thinking, but not the thinking process itself—people do engage in specific activities when they think. These activities may include various kinds of questioning strategies, weighing the validity of evidence, analyzing a particular reading or situation, or writing clearly and persuasively about a particular subject. If these activities can be made explicit, or visible, and are explained and illustrated, then they can also be learned and practiced. Part of critical thinking, therefore, is becoming aware of what you do when you think and learning strategies to help you think more effectively.

Critical thinking, however, also implies a particular frame of mind that is especially suited to active learning. Whereas in other contexts the term *critical* may mean negative or judgmental, here it means self-conscious, curious, and independent. Critical thinkers are self-conscious in that they are aware of how they think and are able to name and monitor the strategies they apply to a range of problems. Critical thinkers are curious in that they try to push beyond the obvious and below the surface of issues, asking questions that extend their knowledge and exploring new pathways and new approaches to problems. Finally, critical thinkers are independent, able to listen to and learn from others, yet also able to develop their own voices and make their own judgments.

This handbook is written especially for students who want to learn some practical strategies for critical thinking and who want to apply those strategies to their own college courses and learning situations. Each of the three sections—on critical reading, critical thinking, and critical writing—identifies and illustrates a range of strategies that can help you develop your abilities to comprehend, connect, and communicate ideas. You learn best by doing, so it is important to apply the strategies in an active way, rather than just read about them. Test them out against your own reading, thinking, and writing problems; practice them and play with them; change them and choose among them. As with other kinds of skill development, the more you persist, the more proficient you will become.

As you begin to use the practical strategies in this handbook, you will quickly see that reading, thinking, and writing are interrelated and overlapping activities. Strategies that help you test assumptions in the thinking process will also help you read more effectively. Similarly, learning how to use context as a strategy for critical reading can, in turn, make you more conscious as a writer of the importance of creating a context for your own ideas and your own readers. As you gain more confidence in applying the strategies, you should feel free to experiment with and adapt them to a variety of problems.

For the most part, you should be able to use this book on your own, transferring the strategies to your own courses, and gradually adding to and developing your critical skills. However, you might also want to practice some of the strategies with a learning or writing partner. No matter whether you are working alone or with a group, it is probably reassuring to know that all of these strategies have actually been used before by other college students. They have all been, in a sense, road-tested. You will no doubt discover that some suit your needs better than others and that some may already be familiar. Still, if there is only one strategy here that makes learning a less passive and more passionate activity for you, then you are already on the way to becoming a stronger, clearer critical thinker.

CRITICAL

READING

APPLYING CONTEXT AS A READING STRATEGY

The first step in becoming an active, critical reader is to realize that reading is not a passive activity: as readers, we are not simply sponges absorbing information and knowledge situated outside us in a text. Rather, as critical readers we create meaning by interacting with a text. This interaction involves such activities as connecting a text to our own experience, discovering patterns in a text, and building relationships among ideas.

The term *text* is used here to refer specifically to written material, either fictional or nonfictional. Such material, whether a short story, poem, a novel, a historical document, or a critical essay, is rooted in a larger context. *Context* can be defined as the situational, cultural, or historical set of circumstances out of which a text grows. For example, the words on this page you are reading are part of a text on critical thinking. The context would include the academic setting you are in, the course you are taking, and current attitudes and ideas about the importance of critical thinking in higher education.

Understanding context is a crucial strategy in the process of critical reading, since context offers a framework from which to begin the process of interpreting a text. Active readers enrich their understanding of a text by drawing upon its context.

To experience for yourself the importance of context in creating meaning for a text, read the following brief passage:

> Lucy noticed that clothes were a popular choice—certain colors, particular items—but sometimes it was just too hot to wear her sweater. Unfortunately, she had failed printing in grade one, and she had never learned to whistle loudly either. Growing a beard was not possible biologically, and she decided she liked the length and color of her hair. In desperation, she tried crossing her fingers on both hands,

but soon realized she couldn't easily eat hot dogs that way. It finally dawned on her, when she was on vacation and reading a newspaper in New Zealand, that she was truly peripheral, but loyal nonetheless.[1]

Although most likely you understand the words and sentences you have just read, it is very difficult to grasp what the passage is about. You may know what it says but not what it means. To create meaning, you need to be able to connect the seemingly unrelated ideas into an understandable pattern. In this case, the text is a riddle because it lacks context, or a frame of reference that allows you to bridge the gaps between the sentences.

Now read the passage again with the following sentence as a guide: "Like many devoted baseball fans, Lucy believed her own actions might help her team win." This sentence provides a context for the passage, and you can draw on your own experience of cheering for a team or your observations of the behavior of fans to build relationships within and among sentences. For example, printing signs and whistling loudly are common forms of fan support. Lucy crosses her fingers because of the superstition that doing so brings luck to her team, and she is eating hot dogs which are always for sale at a ballpark. The puzzle of the final sentence can also be solved with the clues from the context sentence: Lucy is reading a newspaper to find the baseball scores. Presumably, the team at home is winning without her help, so she realizes that her actions cannot really affect the outcome of the games. The best support Lucy can hope to give her team is loyalty.

This exercise should help you discover how important context is as a strategy in the process of reading critically. Context provides valuable clues and sets up expectations that critical readers can then test, revise, or explore in a given text.

How to Determine Context

In the story about Lucy, the context sentence that allows you to create a coherent meaning is provided for you. But where do you look for context when you are expected to read critically with little guidance?

---

1. Adapted from Kristie S. Fleckenstein, "An Appetite for Coherence: Arousing and Fulfilling Desires," *College Composition and Communication* 42, 1991:82–83.

First, it is important to recognize that all texts are inextricably linked to particular situations, cultures, and histories. By situating a text, you will be able to discover valuable contextual information. You can often situate, or locate, a text in time and place by checking its copyright page and by reading the publisher's short notes, or blurbs, about the author and content. Anthologized readings are frequently introduced with notes about authors, and readings are often grouped according to a particular theme or issue. For example, if a selection of essays, short stories, and poems is grouped together under the heading "Family," you can use this context as a strategy to help you find patterns within and among the texts. Before reading the material, you might jot down any ideas or questions you have about kinds of families and family issues and then test your list against the material as you read. The list might resemble this one:

Extended family
Single-parent family
Parent-child conflict
Sibling rivalry
Family values
The ideal family
Divorce
Family violence

How much have ideas about family changed over the years?

What exactly are family values? Are they the same in different cultures?

How closely does the ideal TV family match reality?

Why does the image of the happy family have so much appeal?

From a single heading—"Family"—you can generate a rich context that will help you engage with your reading assignments and better understand them.

A particular context often overlooked by students is academic context, including the discipline being studied. Class discussions and lectures can often provide you with a context for particular readings by raising issues or offering perspectives you might not have considered on your own. Observing how other people connect to an issue or a text is especially valuable because it helps you move beyond a personal or private response to a broader, more active understanding of key issues.

Because most college courses are designed around a particular set of themes or theoretical ideas, they have their own frame of reference. The same is true of academic disciplines or fields of study. Try to use the context of the course itself to situate the readings you are assigned. For example, if you are taking a political science course, you might revise your list about family to include the following issues:

Community as extended family
Nation as family
The rhetoric about family values in recent political campaigns
Daycare as a political issue
National leaders as father figures

Finally, once you have read and understood an essay or short story about family, that knowledge, too, will become part of the context you can apply to further readings.

Illustration

To begin practicing your skills in using context as a reading strategy, read this note that introduces Ruth Rendells's short story "The Orchard Walls":

> Ruth Rendell is one of Britain's top crime novelists. A brilliant storyteller, her ingenious plots, subtle characterizations, and gift for suspense have earned her major literary awards including the Crime Writers Silver Dagger Award in 1985.
>
> "Orchard Walls" is taken from a collection of stories, *The New Girlfriend*, published in 1985. Set in the English countryside during World War II, it recounts the vivid and romantic memories of a young London evacuee whose tragic mistake reveals a sinister and hidden truth.

Before reading the story, consider what expectations you might draw from this context that will help you engage with the text. Some crime is likely to be committed, and there should be an element of mystery. There is also a historical context, and you may have prior knowledge of the fact that, during the bombing of London in World War II, many children were removed from the city to the greater safety of the countryside. Memory, perhaps romance, and a crucial mistake will be important in the storytelling. Already a sense of suspense surrounds the kind of truth that will be revealed.

Now suppose that you are taking a course to learn about effective writing strategies and that this reading is assigned to you under the heading "Narration and Description." What information can you then add to your contextual frame of reference? You might want to list some of the points and questions that occur to you, such as the following:

Look for a central conflict
Is the plot arranged chronologically?
Descriptive details
Narrative point of view

Since the introductory note tells you that Rendell is known for her "ingenious plots," you might even link this information to what you are learning about narrative techniques and be alerted to the possibility of a plot twist or surprise ending. Remember that applying context as a reading strategy allows you to form expectations or make guesses about the text that you can then use to help you discover patterns and create meaning. Now you are ready to read "The Orchard Walls."

THE ORCHARD WALLS

Ruth Rendell

I have never told anyone about this before.

The worst was long over, of course. Intense shame had faded and the knowledge of having made the greatest possible fool of myself. Forty years and more had done their work there. The feeling I had been left with, that I was precocious in a foul and dirty way, that I was unclean, was washed away. I had done my best never to think about it, to blot it all out, never to permit to ring on my inward ear Mrs. Thorn's words:

'How dare you say such a thing! How dare you be so disgusting! At your age, a child, you must be sick in your mind.'

Things would bring it back, the scent of honeysuckle, a brace of bloodied pigeons hanging in a butcher's window, the first cherries of the season. I winced at these things, I grew hot with a shadow of that blush that had set me on fire with shame under the tree, Daniel's hard hand gripping my shoulder, Mrs. Thorn trembling with indignant rage. The memory, never completely exorcised, still had the power to punish the adult for the child's mistake.

Until today.

Having one's childhood trauma cured by an analyst must be like this, only a newspaper has cured mine. The newspaper came through my door and told me I hadn't been disgusting or sick in my mind, I had been right. In the broad facts at least I had been right. All day I have been asking myself what I should do, what action, if any, I should take. At last I have been able to think about it all quite calmly, in tranquillity, to think of Ella and Dennis Clifton without growing hot and ashamed, of Mrs. Thorn with pity and of that lovely lost place with something like nostalgia.

It was a long time ago. I was fourteen. Is that to be a child? They thought so, I thought so myself at the time. But the truth was I was a child and not a child, at one and the same time a paddler in streams, a climber of trees, an expert at cartwheels—and with an imagination full of romantic love. I was in a stage of transition, a pupa, a chrysalis, I was fourteen.

Bombs were falling on London. I had already once been evacuated with my school and come back again to the suburb we lived in that sometimes seemed safe and sometimes not. My parents were afraid for me and that was why they sent me to Inchfield, to the Thorns. I could see the fear in my mother's eyes and it made me uncomfortable.

"Just till the end of August," she said, pleading with me. "It's beautiful there. You could think of it as an extra long summer holiday."

I remembered Hereford and my previous "billet," the strange people, the alien food.

"This will be different. Ella is your own aunt."

She was my mother's sister, her junior by twelve years. There were a brother and sister in between, both living in the north. Ella's husband was a farmer in Suffolk, or had been. He was in the army and his elder brother ran the farm. Later, when Ella was dead and Philip Thorn married again and all I kept of them was that shameful thing I did my best to forget, I discovered that Ella had married Philip when she was seventeen because she was pregnant and in the thirties any alternative to marriage in those circumstances was unthinkable. She had married him and six months later given birth to a dead child. When I went to Inchfield she was still only twenty-five, still childless, living with a brother-in-law and a mother-in-law in the depths of the country, her husband away fighting in North Africa.

I didn't want to go. At fourteen one isn't afraid, one knows one is immortal. After an air raid we used to go about the streets collecting pieces of shrapnel, fragments of shell. The worst thing to me was having to sleep under a Morrison shelter instead of in my bedroom. Having a room of my own again, a place to be private in, was an inducement. I yielded. To this day I don't know if I was invited or if my mother had simply written to say I was coming, that I must come, that they must give me refuge.

It was the second week of June when I went. Daniel Thorn met me at the station at Ipswich. I was wildly romantic, far too romantic, my head full of fantasies and dreams. Knowing I should be met, I expected a pony carriage or even a man on a black stallion leading a chestnut mare for me, though I had never in my life been on a horse. He came in an old Ford van.

We drove to Inchfield through deep green silent lanes—silent, that is, but for the occasional sound of a shot. I thought it must be something to do with the war, without specifying to myself what.

"The war?" said Daniel as if this were something happening ten thousand miles away. He laughed the age-old laugh of the countryman scoring off the townie. "You'll find no war here. That's some chap out after rabbits."

Rabbit was what we were to live on, stewed, roasted, in pies, relieved by wood pigeon. It was a change from London sausages but I have never eaten rabbit since, not once. The characteristic smell of it cooking, experienced once in a friend's kitchen, brought me violent nausea. What a devil's menu that would have been for me, stewed rabbit and cherry pie!

The first sight of the farm enchanted me. The place where I lived in Hereford had been a late-Victorian brick cottage, red and raw and ugly as poverty. I had scarcely seen a house like Cherry Tree Farm except on a calendar. It was long and low and thatched and its two great barns were thatched too. The low green hills and the dark clustering woods hung behind it. And scattered all over the side slopes of grass were the cherry trees, one so close up to the house as to rub its branches against a window pane.

They came out of the front door to meet us, Ella and Mrs. Thorn, and Ella gave me a white, rather cold, cheek to kiss. She didn't smile. She looked bored. It was better therefore than I had expected and worse. Ella was worse and Mrs. Thorn was better. The place was ten times better, tea was like something I hadn't had since before the war, my bedroom was not only nicer than the Morrison shelter, it was nicer than my bedroom at home. Mrs. Thorn took me up there when we had eaten the scones and currant bread and walnut cake.

It was low-ceilinged with the stone-colored studs showing through the plaster. A patchwork quilt was on the bed and the walls were hung with a paper patterned all over with bunches of cherries. I looked out of the window.

"You can't see the cherry trees from here," I said. "Is that why they put cherries on the walls?"

The idea seemed to puzzle her. She was a simple conservative woman. "I don't know about that. That would be rather whimsical."

I was at the back of the house. My window overlooked a trim dull garden of rosebeds cut out in segments of a circle. Mrs. Thorn's own garden, I was later to learn, and tended by herself.

"Who sleeps in the room with the cherry tree?" I said.

"Your auntie." Mrs. Thorn was always to refer to Ella in this way. She was a stickler for respect. "That has always been my son Philip's room."

Always . . . I envied the absent soldier. A tree with branches against one's bedroom window represented to me something down which one could climb and make one's escape, perhaps even without the aid of knotted sheets. I said as much, toning it down for my companion who I guessed would see it in a different light.

"I'm sure he did no such thing," said Mrs. Thorn. "He wasn't that kind of boy."

Those words stamped Philip for me as dull. I wondered why Ella had married him. What had she seen in this unromantic chap, five years her senior, who hadn't been the kind of boy to climb down trees out of his bedroom window? Or climb up them, come to that . . .

She was beautiful. For the first Christmas of the war I had been given *Picturegoer Annual* in which was a full-page photograph of Hedy Lamarr. Ella looked just like her. She had the same perfect features, dark hair, other-worldly eyes fixed on far horizons. I can see her now— I can *permit* myself to see her—as she was then, thin, long-legged, in the floral cotton dress with collar and cuffs and narrow belt that would be fashionable again today. Her hair was pinned up in a roll off her forehead, the rest left hanging to her shoulders in loose curls, mouth painted like raspberry jam, eyes as nature made them, large, dark, alight with some emotion I was years from analyzing. I think now it was compounded of rebellion and longing and desire.

Sometimes in the early evenings she would disappear upstairs and then Mrs. Thorn would say in a respectful voice that she had gone to write to Philip. We used to listen to the wireless. Of course no one knew exactly where Philip was but we all had a good idea he was somehow involved in the attempts to relieve Tobruk. At news times Mrs. Thorn became very tense. Once, to my embarrassment, she made a choking sound and left the room, covering her eyes with her hand. Ella switched off the set.

"You ought to be in bed," she said to me. "When I was your age I was always in bed by eight."

I envied and admired her, even though she was never particularly nice to me and seldom spoke except to say I "ought" to be doing something or other. Did she look at this niece, not much more than ten years younger than herself, and see what she herself had thrown away, a future of hope, a chance of living?

I spent very little time with her. It was Mrs. Thorn who took me shopping with her to Ipswich, who talked to me while she did the baking, who knitted and taught me to knit. There was no wool to be had so we unpicked old jumpers and washed the wool and carded it and started again. I was with her most of the time. It was either that or being on my own. No doubt there were children of my own age in the village I might have got to know but the village was two miles away. I was allowed to go out for walks but not to ride the only bicycle they had.

"It's too large for you, it's a twenty-eight inch," Mrs. Thorn said. "Besides, it's got a crossbar."

I said I could easily swing my leg behind the saddle like a man.

"Not while you're staying with me."

I didn't understand. "I wouldn't hurt myself." I said what I said to my mother. "I wouldn't come to any harm."

"It isn't ladylike," said Mrs. Thorn, and that was that.

Those things mattered a lot to her. She stopped me turning cartwheels on the lawn when Daniel was about, even though I wore shorts. Then she made me wear a skirt. But she was kind, she paid me a lot of attention. If I had had to depend on Ella or the occasional word from Daniel I might have looked forward more eagerly to my parent's fortnightly visits than I did.

After I had been there two or three weeks the cherries began to turn color. Daniel, coming upon me looking at them, said they were an old variety called Inchfield White Heart.

"There used to be a cherry festival here," he said. "The first Sunday after July the twelfth it was. There'd be dancing and a supper, you'd have enjoyed yourself. Still, we never had one last year and we're not this and somehow I don't reckon there'll ever be a cherry festival again what with this old war."

He was a yellow-haired, red-complexioned Suffolk man, big and thickset. His wide mouth, sickle-shaped, had its corners permanently turned upwards. It wasn't a smile though and he was seldom cheerful. I never heard him laugh. He used to watch people in rather a disconcerting way, Ella especially. And when guests came to the house, Dennis Clifton or Mrs. Leithman or some of the farming people they knew, he would sit and watch them, seldom contributing a word.

One evening, when I was coming back from a walk, I saw Ella and Dennis Clifton kissing in the wood.

Dennis Clifton wasn't a farmer. He had been in the R.A.F., had been a fighter pilot in the Battle of Britain but had received some sort of head injury, been in hospital and was now on leave at home recuperating. He must have been very young, no more than twenty-two or three.

While he was ill his mother, with whom he had lived and who had been a friend of Mrs. Thorn's, had died and left him her pretty little Georgian house in Inchfield. He was often at the farm, ostensibly to see his mother's old friend.

After these visits Daniel used to say, "He'll soon be back in the thick of it," or "It won't be long before he's up there in his Spitfire. He can't wait."

This made me watch him too, looking for signs of impatience to return to the R.A.F. His hands shook sometimes, they trembled like an old man's. He too was fair-haired and blue-eyed, yet there was all the difference in the world between his appearance and Daniel's. Film stars set my standard of beauty and I thought he looked like Leslie Howard playing Ashley Wilkes. He was tall and thin and sensitive and his eyes were sad. Daniel watched him and Ella sat silent and I read my book while he talked very kindly and encouragingly to Mrs. Thorn about her son Philip, about how confident he was Philip would be all right, would survive, and while he talked his eyes grew sadder and more veiled.

No, I have imagined that, not remembered it. It is in the light of what I came to know that I have imagined it. He was simply considerate and kind like the well-brought-up young man he was.

I had been in the river. There was a place about a mile upstream they called the weir where for a few yards the banks were built up with concrete below a shallow fall. A pool about four feet deep had formed there and on hot days I went bathing in it. Mrs. Thorn would have stopped me if she had known but she didn't know. She didn't even know I had a bathing costume with me.

The shortest way back was through the wood. I heard a shot and then another from up in the meadows. Daniel was out after pigeons. The wood was dim and cool, full of soft twitterings, feathers rustling against dry leaves. The bluebells were long past but dog's mercury was in flower, a white powdering, and the air was scented with honeysuckle. Another shot came, further off but enough to shatter peace, and there was a rush of wings as pigeons took flight. Through the black trunks of trees and the lacework of their branches I could see the yellow sky and the sun burning in it, still an hour off setting.

Ella was leaning against the trunk of a chestnut, looking up into Dennis Clifton's face. He had his hands pressed against the trunk, on either side of her head. If she had ever been nice to me, if he had ever said more than hallo, I think I might have called out to them. I didn't call and in a moment I realized the last thing they would want was to be seen.

I stayed where I was. I watched them. Oh, I was in no way a voyeur.

There was nothing lubricious in it, nothing of curiosity, still less a wish to catch them out. I was overwhelmed rather by the romance of it, ravished by wonder. I watched him kiss her. He took his hands down and put his arms round her and kissed her so that their faces were no longer visible, only his fair head and her dark hair and their locked straining shoulders. I caught my breath and shivered in the warm half-light, in the honeysuckle air.

They left the place before I did, walking slowly away in the direction of the road, arms about each other's waists. In the room at Cherry Tree Farm they still called the parlor Mrs. Thorn and Daniel were sitting, listening to the wireless, drinking tea. No more than five minutes afterwards Ella came in. I had seen what I had seen but if I hadn't, wouldn't I still have thought her looks extraordinary, her shining eyes and the flush on her white cheeks, the willow leaf in her hair and the bramble clinging to her skirt?

Daniel looked at her. There was blood in his fingernails, though he had scrubbed his hands. It brought me a flicker of nausea. Ella put her fingers through her hair, plucked out the leaf and went upstairs.

"She is going up to write to Philip," said Mrs. Thorn.

Why wasn't I shocked? Why wasn't I horrified? I was only fourteen and I came from a conventional background. Adultery was something committed by people in the Bible. I suppose I could say I had seen no more than a kiss and adultery didn't enter into it. Yet I knew it did. With no experience, with only the scantiest knowledge, I sensed that this love had its full consummation. I knew Ella was married to a soldier who was away fighting for his country. I even knew that my parents would think behavior such as hers despicable if not downright wicked. But I cared for none of that. To me it was romance, it was Lancelot and Guinevere, it was a splendid and beautiful adventure that was happening to two handsome young people—as one day it might happen to me.

I was no go-between. For them I scarcely existed. I received no words or smiles, still less messages to be carried. They had the phone, anyway, they had cars. But though I took no part in their love affair and wasn't even with accuracy able to calculate the times when it was conducted, it filled my thoughts. Outwardly I followed the routine of days I had arranged for myself and Mrs. Thorn had arranged for me, but my mind was occupied with Dennis and Ella, assessing what meeting places they would use, imagining their conversations—their vows of undying love—and re-creating with cinematic variations that kiss.

My greatest enjoyment, my finest hours of empathy, were when he called. I watched the two of them as intently then as Daniel did.

Sometimes I fancied I caught between them a glance of longing and once I actually witnessed something more, an encounter between them in the passage when Ella came from the kitchen with the tea tray and Dennis had gone to fetch something from his car for Mrs. Thorn. Unseen by them, I stood in the shadow between the grandfather clock and the foot of the stairs. I heard him whisper:

"Tonight? Same place?"

She nodded, her eyes wide. I saw him put his hand on her shoulder in a slow caress as he went past her.

I slept badly those nights. It had become very hot. Mrs. Thorn made sure I was in bed by nine and there was no way of escaping from the house after that without being seen by her. I envied Ella with a tree outside her window down which it would be easy to climb and escape. I imagined going down to the river in the moonlight, walking in the wood, perhaps seeing my lovers in some trysting place. My lovers, whose breathy words and laden glances exalted me and rarefied the overheated air . . .

The cherries were turning pale yellow with a blush coming to their cheeks. It was the first week of July, the week the war came to Inchfield and a German bomber, lost and off course, unloaded a stick of bombs in one of the Thorns' fields.

No one was hurt, though a cow got killed. We went to look at the mess in the meadow, the crater and the uprooted tree. Daniel shook his fist at the sky. The explosions had made a tremendous noise and we were all sensitive after that to any sudden sound. Even the crack of Daniel's shotgun made his mother jump.

The heat had turned sultry and clouds obscured our blue skies, though no rain fell. Mrs. Leithman, coming to tea as she usually did once in the week, told us she fancied each roll of thunder was another bomb. We hardly saw Ella, she was always up in her room or out somewhere—out with Dennis, of course. I speculated about them, wove fantasies around them, imagined Philip Thorn killed in battle and thereby setting them free. So innocent was I, living in more innocent or at least more puritanical times, that the possibility of this childless couple being divorced never struck me. Nor did I envisage Dennis and Ella married to each other but only continuing forever their perilous enchanting idyll. I even found Juliet's lines for them—Juliet who was my own age—and whispered to myself that the orchard walls are high and hard to climb and the place death, considering who thou art . . . Once, late at night when I couldn't sleep and sat in my window, I saw the shadowy figure of Dennis Clifton emerge from the deep darkness at the side of the house and leave by the gate out of the rose garden.

But the destruction of it all and my humiliation were drawing nearer. I had settled down there, I had begun to be happy. The truth is, I suppose, that I identified with Ella and in my complex fantasies it was I, compounded with Juliet, that Dennis met and embraced and touched and loved. My involvement was much deeper than that of an observer.

When it came the shot sounded very near. It woke me up as such a sound might not have done before the bombs. I wondered what prey Daniel could go in search of at this hour, for the darkness was deep, velvety and still. The crack which had split the night and jarred the silence wasn't repeated. I went back to sleep and slept till past dawn.

I got up early as I did most mornings, came downstairs in the quiet of the house, the hush of a fine summer morning, and went outdoors. Mrs. Thorn was in the kitchen, frying fat bacon and duck eggs for the men. I didn't know if it was all right for me to do this or if all the cherries were reserved for some mysterious purpose, but as I went towards the gate I reached up and picked a ripe one from a dipping branch. It was the crispest sweetest cherry I have ever tasted, though I must admit I have eaten few since then. I pushed the stone into the earth just inside the gates. Perhaps it germinated and grew. Perhaps quite an old tree that has borne many summer loads of fruit now stands at the entrance to Cherry Tree Farm.

As it happened, of all their big harvest, that was the only cherry I was ever to eat there. Coming back half an hour later, I pushed open the gate and stood for a moment looking at the farmhouse over whose sunny walls and roof the shadows of the trees lay in a slanted leafy pattern. I looked at the big tree, laden with red-gold fruit, that rubbed its branches against Ella's window. In its boughs, halfway up, in a fork a yard or two from the glass, hung the body of a man.

In the hot sunshine I felt icy cold. I remember the feeling to this day, the sensation of being frozen by a cold that came from within while outside me the sun shone and a thrush sang and the swallows dipped in and out under the eaves. My eyes seemed fixed, staring in the hypnosis of shock and fear at the fair-haired dangling man, his head thrown back in the agony of death there outside Ella's bedroom window.

At least I wasn't hysterical. I resolved I must be calm and adult. My teeth were chattering. I walked stiffly into the kitchen and there they all were, round the table, Daniel and the two men and Ella and, at the head of it, Mrs. Thorn pouring tea.

I meant to go quietly up to her and whisper it. I couldn't. To get myself there without running, stumbling, shouting, had used up all the control I had. The words rushed out in a loud ragged bray and I remember holding up my hands, my fists clenched.

"Mr Clifton's been shot. He's been shot, he's dead. His body's in the cherry tree outside Ella's window!"

There was silence. But first a clatter as of knives and forks dropped, of cups rattled into saucers, of chairs scraped. Then this utter stricken silence. I have never—not in all the years since then—seen anyone go as white as Ella went. She was as white as paper and her eyes were black holes. A brick color suffused Daniel's face. He swore. He used words that made me shrink and draw back and shiver and stare from one to the other of the horrible, horrified faces.

Mrs. Thorn was the first to speak, her voice cold with anger.

"How dare you say such a thing! How dare you be so disgusting! At your age—you must be sick in your mind."

Daniel had jumped up. He took me roughly by the arm. But his grasp wasn't firm, the hand was shaking the way Dennis's shook. He manhandled me out there, his mother scuttling behind us. We were still five or six yards from the tree when I saw. The hot blood came into my face and throbbed under my skin. I looked at the cloth face, the yellow wool hair—our own unpicked carded wool—the stuffed sacking body, the cracked boots . . .

Icy with indignation, Mrs. Thorn said, "Haven't you ever seen a scarecrow before?"

I cried out desperately as if, even in the face of this evidence, I could still prove them wrong, "But scarecrows are in fields!"

"Not in this part of the world." Daniel's voice was thin and hoarse. He couldn't have looked more gaunt, more shocked, if it had really been Dennis Clifton in that tree. "In this part of the world we put them in cherry trees. I put it there last night. I put *them* there." And he pointed at what I had passed but never seen, the man in the tree by the wall, the man in the tree in the middle of the green lawn.

I went back to the house and up to my room and lay on the bed, prone and silent with shame. The next day was Saturday and my parents were coming. They would tell them and I should be taken home in disgrace. In the middle of the day Mrs. Thorn came to the door and said to come down to lunch. She was a changed woman, hard and dour. I had never heard the expression 'to draw aside one's skirts' but later on when I did I recognized that this was what she had done to me. Her attitude to me was as if I were some sort of psychopath.

We had lunch alone, only I didn't really have any, I couldn't eat. Just as we were finishing, I pushing aside my laden plate, Daniel came in and sat down and said they had all talked about it and they thought it would be best if I went home with my parents on the following day.

"Of course I shall tell them exactly what you said and what you inferred," said Mrs. Thorn. "I shall tell them how you insulted your auntie."

Daniel, who wasn't trembling any more or any redder in the face than usual, considered this for a moment in silence. Then he said unexpectedly—or unexpectedly to me, "No, we won't, Mother, we won't do that. No point in that. The fewer know the better. You've got to think of Ella's reputation."

"I won't have her here," his mother said.

"No, I agree with that. She can tell them she's homesick or I'll say it's too much for you, having her here."

Ella hid herself away all that day.

"She has her letter to write to Philip," said Mrs. Thorn.

In the morning she was at the table with the others. Daniel made an announcement. He had been down to the village and heard that Dennis Clifton was back in the Air Force, he had rejoined his squadron.

"He'll soon be back in the thick of it," he said.

Ella sat with bowed head, working with restless fingers a slice of bread into a heap of crumbs. Her face was colorless, lacking her usual make-up. I don't remember ever hearing another word from her.

I packed my things. My parents made no demur about taking me back with them. Starved of love, sickened by the love of others, I clung to my father. The scarecrows grinned at us as we got into the van behind Daniel. I can see them now—I can permit myself to see them now—spreadeagled in the trees, protecting the reddening fruit, so lifelike that even the swallows swooped in wider arcs around them.

In the following spring Ella died giving birth to another dead child. My mother cried, for Ella had been her little sister. But she was shy about giving open expression to her grief. She and my father were anxious to keep from me, or for that matter anyone else, that it was a good fifteen months since Philip Thorn had been home on leave. What became of Daniel and his mother I never knew, I didn't want to know. I couldn't avoid hearing that Philip had married again and his new wife was a niece of Mrs. Leithman's.

Only a meticulous reader of newspapers would have spotted the paragraph. I am in the habit or reading every line, with the exception of the sports news, and I spotted this item tucked away between an account of sharp practice in local government and the suicide of a financier. I read it. The years fell away and the facts exonerated me. I know I must do something, I wondered what, I have been thinking of it all day, but now I know I must tell this story to the coroner. My story, my mistake, Daniel's rage.

An agricultural worker had come upon an unexploded bomb on the farm land near Inchfield in Suffolk. It was thought to be one of a stick of bombs dropped there in 1941. Excavations in the area had brought to light a skeleton thought to be that of a young man who had met his death at about the same time. A curious fact was that shotgun pellets had been found in the cavity of the skull.

The orchard walls are high and hard to climb. And the place death considering who thou art, if any of my kinsmen find thee here . . .

_____

After reading the story, take a few minutes to consider the ways in which context informed your reading. The historical context of London's evacuation of children to the countryside probably helped you understand the young girl's loneliness, her subsequent fascination with the lovers, and her ignorance of scarecrows that culminate in her belief that Dennis Clifton has been shot. You probably also noted the importance of memory in the arrangement of the plot and in two recurring patterns of description: the shooting of rabbits in the country, and the cherry trees. Suspense and a sense of mystery are also enhanced by the plot arrangement. As readers, we are told of the girl's shame and bewilderment immediately but are not certain what her mistake is until close to the story's ending. Not until the significance of the newspaper story is explained is it clear that the mistake ironically reveals the truth of murder, after all. An expectation that the story would reveal a crime and a hidden truth makes the surprise ending particularly satisfying.

The fact that critical readers create meaning by interacting with a text can make each reading of the text a new experience. If you read "The Orchard Walls" a second time with a different contextual frame of reference in mind, you are likely to notice and emphasize different elements in the text and thus construct different meanings. For example, suppose the story was assigned in the context of a course or theme dealing with adult and child relations. In this case, you would probably give much greater weight in your reading to the differing adult and child perspectives on adultery, and the girl's needless years of shame caused by the lies and fears of adults.

Finally, while in the act of reading, you may discover a context that you can explore to deepen your understanding. The text itself can reveal a meaningful context. In this case, the title of the story, the narrator's explicit reference to Juliet, and her quoting of Juliet's lines to Romeo are intended to help you make intertextual links. When read in the context of *Romeo and Juliet,* "The Orchard Walls" seems to be a modern retelling of a tale about star-crossed lovers and the menace of Daniel, who is determined to preserve family honor. Thus, an added benefit of applying context as a critical reading strategy is that it frees you from the tyranny of finding "the right answer." By constructing a range of meanings, you will better understand your role as critical reader interacting with a text.

READING WITH A PURPOSE, FOR PURPOSE

Personal experience, general knowledge, values, and opinions are part of the context readers bring to text. In the process of creating meaning, the connecting of new information to prior knowledge is an important first step. However, critical reading also requires an active reader to move beyond a personal response or a statement of personal preference—"I liked this" or "I didn't like this"—to a more reasoned critical judgment based on an awareness of rhetorical strategies. For instance, the reader might conclude: "I liked this *because* the author's purpose was clearly stated and well supported." There are many rhetorical strategies available to writers, but every piece of writing is motivated by a major purpose or set of purposes. If you can determine what an author wants to achieve and why, you can then measure how well an author has achieved those goals. Thus, reading with a definite goal, to determine an author's purpose, is an effective strategy to use in making critical responses to a text.

The Reader's Purpose

In applying this strategy successfully, first consider your own purposes for reading. Sometimes you read simply for pleasure or to gather straightforward information such as directions, in which case you can afford to be relatively passive. In an academic setting, students often read material they expect to be tested on later; if that is your situation and if you are reading with the purpose of exam writing in mind, you may feel compelled to memorize large chunks of facts and even whole sentences. You may also read to find supporting evidence for an argument you are writing and consequently skim over or fail to notice information that contradicts your position. In other words, your purpose for reading can shape your response, and it can influence where you direct your attention.

A major advantage of reading to determine an author's purpose is that you are likely to gain a better grasp of a text. Experienced critical readers know that an author's major purpose often determines content—that is, what might be included or excluded from a text—and how content might be organized. In addition, reading for purpose allows you to determine a hierarchy among parts of a text. Once you discover the author's main statement of purpose, or controlling thesis, you should find that the information that follows relates to it. By focusing on purpose, you are much more likely to recall an author's main points than if you try to memorize everything.

Finally, reading for purpose may help you determine, refine, or revise your own values and points of view. When our own beliefs are challenged, we sometimes reject contrary arguments too quickly. However, by reading for an author's purpose, you increase the likelihood of giving a text a fair hearing, of reading with an open mind, and of formulating a critical response based on the text's own merits or flaws.

The Writer's Purpose

Although purpose is often referred to as a singular concept, an author may well have more than one purpose for writing. Even in books, articles, and essays with a dominant or explicitly stated purpose, other, sometimes implicit, goals often play a role in shaping the text. For example, you might argue that Ruth Rendell's primary purpose in writing "The Orchard Walls" is to reveal the passions and set of circumstances that lead to murder, but other purposes, such as entertaining the reader or creating suspense, also play a part in how she tells the story. Therefore, if you look for a set of interrelated purposes, sometimes called a web of purpose,[2] your interaction with the text will be richer and you need not worry unduly about fastening on the "right" purpose.

2. Linda Flower, "The Construction of Purpose in Writing and Reading," *College English* 50, 1988:531.

The following list includes some of the general purposes an author may have for writing:

To inform
To explain
To illustrate
To entertain
To speculate or explore
To persuade—refute an idea, support a cause, promote change, and so on

Even from this very basic, generic list, you can see how purposes must necessarily overlap and interrelate. Most nonfiction readings assigned at the college level, for example, are persuasive and based on argument. An author can scarcely hope to persuade a reader without also explaining or illustrating the argument. Similarly, fiction often entertains us precisely because it explores human motivations and emotions or illustrates an abstract idea through a particular set of events and dramatic conflicts.

To apply reading for purpose as an effective strategy, then, you need to look for an interrelated set of goals and intentions, which are often located in the opening paragraph of an article, or, in the case of a longer piece of writing, the opening chapter or introduction. Whether one of these purposes becomes dominant can often be determined as you continue to read and begin to see relationships among ideas and paragraphs. A careful reading of the final paragraphs or summary chapter, where an author often restates major points, may provide a further test for purpose. This information can then guide you in formulating a critical response.

Illustration

Diane Barthel's essay "A Gentleman and a Consumer" is taken from her book *Putting on Appearances: Gender and Advertising,* published in 1988. This essay is also included in an anthology, *Gender Images,* used in college level composition courses. The anthology's context notes alert the reader to expect information as to how advertising images sell not merely products, but attitudes and definitions of gender: how men and women are seen in American culture and how they are expected to behave. With this context as a guide, read the first few paragraphs of Barthel's essay and see if you can determine the set of purposes and goals she is using to direct the reader's attention and organize her information. You are looking for major points and controlling ideas.

A GENTLEMAN AND A CONSUMER

Diane Barthel

T here are no men's beauty and glamour magazines with circulations even approaching those of the women's magazine. . . . The very idea of men's beauty magazines may strike one as odd. In our society men traditionally were supposed to make the right appearance, to be well groomed and neatly tailored. What they were *not* supposed to do was to be overly concerned with their appearance, much less vain about their beauty. That was to be effeminate, and not a "real man." Male beauty was associated with homosexuals, and "real men" had to show how red-blooded they were by maintaining a certain distance from fashion.

Perhaps the best-known male fashion magazine is *GQ* founded in 1957 and with a circulation of 446,000 in 1986. More recently, we have seen the launching of *YMF* and *Young Black Male,* which in 1987 still have few advertising pages. *M* magazine, founded in 1983, attracts an audience "a cut above" that of *GQ.*[1]

Esquire magazine, more venerable (founded in 1933), is classified as a general interest magazine. Although it does attract many women readers, many of the columns and features and much of the advertising are definitely directed toward attracting the attention of the male readers, who still make up the overwhelming majority of the readership.

The highest circulations for men's magazines are for magazines specializing either in sex (*Playboy,* circulation 4.1 million; *Penthouse,* circulation nearly 3.8 million; and *Hustler,* circulation 1.5 million) or sports (*Sports Illustrated,* circulation 2.7 million).[2] That these magazines share an emphasis on power—either power over women or over other men on the playing field—should not surprise. In fact, sociologist John Gagnon would argue that sex and sports now represent the major fields in which the male role, as defined by power, is played out, with physical power in work, and even in warfare, being less important than it was before industrialization and technological advance.[3]

If we are looking for comparative evidence as to how advertisements define gender roles for men and women, we should not then see the male role as defined primarily through beauty and fashion. This seems an obvious point, but it is important to emphasize how different cultural attitudes toward both the social person and the physical body shape the gender roles of men and women. These cultural attitudes are changing, and advertisements are helping to legitimate the use of beauty products and an interest in fashion for men, as we shall see. As advertisements directed toward women are beginning to use male imagery, so too advertisements for men occasionally use imagery resembling that found in advertisements directed toward women. We are speaking of two *modes*, then. As Baudrillard writes, these modes "do not result from the differentiated nature of the two sexes, but from the differential logic of the system. The relationship of the Masculine and the Feminine to real men and women is relatively arbitrary."[4] Increasingly today, men and women use both modes. The two great terms of opposition (Masculine and Feminine) still, however, structure the forms that consumption takes; they provide identities for products and consumers.

Baudrillard agrees that the feminine model encourages a woman to please herself, to encourage a certain complacency and even narcissistic solicitude. But by pleasing herself, it is understood that she will also please others, and that she will be chosen. "She never enters into direct competition. . . . If she is beautiful, that is to say, if this woman is a woman, she will be chosen. If the man is a man, he will choose his woman as he would other objects/signs (HIS car, HIS woman, HIS eau de toilette)."[5]

Whereas the feminine model is based on passivity, complacency, and narcissism, the masculine model is based on exactingness and choice.

> All of masculine advertising insists on rule, on choice, in
> terms of rigor and inflexible minutiae. He does not neglect
> a detail . . . It is not a question of just letting things go, or
> of taking pleasure in something, but rather of distinguish-
> ing himself. To know how to choose, and not to fail at it, is
> here the equivalent of the military and puritanical virtues:
> intransigence, decision, "virtus."[6]

This masculine model, these masculine virtues, are best reflected in the many car advertisements. There, the keywords are masculine terms: *power, performance, precision*. Sometimes the car is a woman, responding to the touch and will of her male driver, after attracting him with her sexy body. "Pure shape, pure power, pure Z. It turns you on." But, as the juxtaposition of shape and power in this advertisement suggests, the car is not simply other; it is also an extension of the owner. As he turns it on, he turns himself on. Its power is his power; through it, he will be able to overpower other men and impress and seduce women.

How well does it perform?
How well can you drive? (Merkur XR4Ti)
The 1987 Celica GT-S has the sweeping lines and aggressive stance that promise performance. And Celica keeps its word.

Renault GTA:
Zero to sixty to zero in 13.9 sec.
It's the result of a performance philosophy where acceleration and braking are equally important.
There's a new Renault sports sedan called GTA. Under its slick monochromatic skin is a road car with a total performance attitude. . . . It's our hot new pocket rocket.

In this last example, the car, like the driver, has a total performance attitude. That is what works. The slick monochromatic skin, like the Bond Street suit, makes a good first impression. But car, like owner, must have what it takes, must be able to go the distance faster and better than the competition. This point is explicitly made in advertisements in which the car becomes a means through which this masculine competition at work is extended in leisure. Some refer directly to the manly sport of auto-racing: "The Mitsubishi Starion ESI-R. Patiently crafted to ignite your imagination. Leaving little else to say except . . . gentlemen, start your engines." Others refer to competition in the business world: "To move ahead fast in this world, you've got to have connections. The totally new Corolla FX 16 GT-S has the right ones." Or in life in general. "It doesn't take any [Japanese characters] from anyone. It won't stand for any guff from 300ZX. Or RX-7. Introducing Conquest Tsi, the new turbo sport coupe designed and built by Mitsubishi in Japan." Or Ferrari, which says simply, "We are the competition." In this competition between products, the owners become almost superfluous. But the advertisements, of course, suggest that the qualities of the car will reflect the qualities of the owner, as opposed to the purely abstract, apersonal quality of money needed for purchase. Thus, like the would-be owner, the BMW also demonstrates a "relentless refusal to compromise." It is for "those who thrive on a maximum daily requirement of high performance." While the BMW has the business attitude of the old school ("aggression has never been expressed with such dignity"), a Beretta suggests what it takes to survive today in the shark-infested waters of Wall Street. In a glossy three-page cover foldout, a photograph of a shark's fin cutting through indigo waters is accompanied by the legend "Discover a new species from today's Chevrolet." The following two pages show a sleek black Beretta similarly cutting through water and, presumably, through the competition: "Not just a new car, but a new species . . . with a natural instinct for the road . . . Aggressive stance. And a bold tail lamp. See it on the road and you won't soon forget. Drive it, and you never will."

And as with men, so with cars. "Power corrupts. Absolute power corrupts absolutely" (Maserati). Not having the money to pay for a Maserati, to corrupt and be corrupted, is a source of embarrassment. Advertisements reassure the consumer that he need not lose face in this manly battle. Hyundai promises, "It's affordable. (But you'd never know it.)"

> On first impression, the new Hyundai Excel GLS Sedan might seem a trifle beyond most people's means. But that's entirely by design. Sleek European design, to be exact.

Many advertisements suggest sexual pleasure and escape, as in "Pure shape, pure power, pure Z. It turns you on." Or "The all-new Chrysler Le Baron. Beauty . . . with a passion for driving." The Le Baron may initially suggest a beautiful female, with its "image of arresting beauty" and its passion "to drive. And drive it does!" But it *is* "Le Baron," not "La Baronness." And the advertisement continues to emphasize how it *attacks* [emphasis mine] the road with a high torque, 2.5 fuel-injected engine. And its turbo option can blur the surface of any passing lane." Thus the object of the pleasure hardly has to be female if it is beautiful or sleek. The car is an extension of the male that conquers and tames the (female) road: "Positive-response suspension will calm the most demanding roads." The car becomes the ultimate lover when, like the Honda Prelude, it promises to combine power, "muscle," with finesse. Automobile advertisements thus play with androgyny and sexuality; the pleasure is in the union and confusion of form and movement, sex and speed. As in any sexual union, there is ultimately a merging of identities, rather than rigid maintenance of their separation. Polymorphous perverse? Perhaps. But it sells.

Though power, performance, precision as a complex of traits find their strongest emphasis in automobile advertisements, they also appear as selling points for products as diverse as shoes, stereos, and sunglasses. The car performs on the road, the driver performs for women, even in the parking lot, as Michelin suggests in its two-page spread showing a male from the waist down resting on his car and chatting up a curvaceous female: "It performs great. And looks great. So, it not only stands out on the road. But in the parking lot. Which is one more place you're likely to discover how beautifully it can handle the curves"(!).

As media analyst Todd Gitlin points out, most of the drivers shown in advertisements are young white males, loners who become empowered by the car that makes possible their escape from the everyday. Gitlin stresses the advertisements' "emphasis on surface, the blankness of the protagonist; his striving toward self-sufficiency, to the point of displacement from the recognizable world."[7] Even the Chrysler advertisements that coopt Bruce Springsteen's "Born in the USA" for their "Born in America" campaign lose in the process the original political message, "ripping off Springsteen's angry anthem, smoothing it into a Chamber of Commerce ditty as shots of just plain productive-looking folks, black and white . . . whiz by in a montage-made community." As Gitlin comments, "None of Springsteen's losers need apply—or rather, if only they would roll up their sleeves and see what good company they're in, they wouldn't feel like losers any longer."[8]

This is a world of patriarchal order in which the individual male can and must challenge the father. He achieves identity by breaking loose of the structure and breaking free of the pack. In the process he recreates the order and reaffirms the myth of masculine independence. Above all, he demonstrates that he knows what he wants; he is critical, demanding, and free from the constraints of others. What he definitely does not want, and goes to some measure to avoid, is to appear less than masculine, in any way weak, frilly, feminine.

Avoiding the Feminine

Advertisers trying to develop male markets for products previously associated primarily with women must overcome the taboo that only women wear moisturizer, face cream, hair spray, or perfume. They do this by overt reference to masculine symbols, language, and imagery, and sometimes by confronting the problem head-on.

There is not so much of a problem in selling products to counteract balding—that traditionally has been recognized as a male problem (a bald woman is a sexual joke that is not particularly amusing to the elderly). But other hair products are another story, as the March 1987 *GQ* cover asks, "Are you man enough for mousse?" So the advertisements must make their products seem manly, as with S-Curl's "wave and curl kit" offering "The Manly Look" on its manly model dressed in business suit and carrying a hard hat (a nifty social class compromise), and as in college basketball sportscaster Al McGuire's testimonial for Consort hair spray:

> "Years ago, if someone had said to me, 'Hey Al, do you use hair spray?' I would have said, 'No way, baby!'"

"That was before I tried Consort Pump."
"Consort adds extra control to my hair without looking
stiff or phony. Control that lasts clean into overtime and
post-game interviews . . ."
Grooming Gear for Real Guys. *Consort.*

Besides such "grooming gear" as perms and hair sprays, Real Guys
use "skin supplies" and "shaving resources." They adopt a "survival
strategy" to fight balding, and the "Fila philosophy"—"products with
a singular purpose: performance"—for effective "bodycare." If they
wear scent, it smells of anything *but* flowers: musk, woods, spices, cit-
rus, and surf are all acceptable. And the names must be manly, whether
symbolizing physical power ("Brut") or financial power ("Giorgio VIP
Special Reserve," "The Baron. A distinctive fragrance for men,"
"Halston—For the privileged few").

As power/precision/performance runs as a theme throughout
advertising to men, so too do references to the business world. Cars, as
we have seen, promise to share their owner's professional attitude and
aggressive drive to beat out the competition. Other products similarly
reflect the centrality of business competition to the male gender role.
And at the center of this competition itself, the business suit.

At the onset of your business day, you choose the suit or
sportcoat that will position you front and center . . .
The Right Suit can't guarantee he'll see it your way. The
wrong suit could mean not seeing him at all.

Along with the Right Suit, the right shirt. "You want it every time you
reach across the conference table, or trade on the floor, or just move
about. You want a shirt that truly fits, that is long enough to stay put
through the most active day, even for the taller gentleman." The busi-
nessman chooses the right cologne—Grey Flannel, or perhaps Quorum.
He wears a Gucci "timepiece" as he conducts business on a cordless telephone from his poolside—or prefers the "dignity in styling" promised
by Raymond Weil watches, "a beautiful way to dress for success."

Men's products connect status and success; the right products show
that you have the right stuff, that you're one of them. In the 1950s
C. Wright Mills described what it took to get ahead, to become part of
the "power elite":

The fit survive, and fitness means, not formal competence
. . . but conformity with the criteria of those who have
already succeeded. To be compatible with the top men is to

act like them, to look like them, to think like them: to be of and for them—or at least to display oneself to them in such a way as to create that impression. This, in fact, is what is meant by "creating"—a well-chosen word—"a good impression." This is what is meant—and nothing else—by being a "sound man," as sound as a dollar.[9]

Today, having what it takes includes knowing "the difference between dressed, and well dressed" (Bally shoes). It is knowing that "what you carry says as much about you as what you put inside it" (Hartmann luggage). It is knowing enough to imitate Doug Fout, "member of one of the foremost equestrian families in the country."

Because of our adherence to quality and the natural shoul-der tradition, Southwick clothing was adopted by the Fout family years ago. Clearly, they have as much appreciation for good lines in a jacket as they do in a thoroughbred.

There it is, old money. There is no substitute for it, really, in business or in advertising, where appeals to tradition form one of the mainstays guaranteeing men that their choices are not overly fashionable or femi-nine, not working class or cheap, but, rather, correct, in good form, above criticism. If, when they achieve this status of gentlemanly per-fection, then, the advertisement suggests, they may be invited to join the club.

When only the best of associations will do

Recognizing style as the requisite for membership, dis-cerning men prefer the natural shoulder styling of Racquet Club. Meticulously tailored in pure wool, each suit and sportcoat is the ultimate expression of the clubman's classic good taste.

Ralph Lauren has his Polo University Club, and Rolex picks up on the polo theme by sponsoring the Rolex Gold Cup held at the Palm Beach Polo and Country Club, where sixteen teams and sixty-four players competed for "the pure honor of winning, the true glory of victory":

It has added new lustre to a game so ancient, its history is lost in legend. Tamerlane is said to have been its patriarch. Darius's Persian cavalry, we're told, played it. It was the national sport of 16th-century India, Egypt, China, and Japan. The British rediscovered and named it in 1857.

The linking of polo and Rolex is uniquely appropriate.
Both sponsor and sport personify rugged grace. Each is an
arbiter of the art of timing.

In the spring of 1987, there was another interesting club event—or
non-event. The prestigious New York University Club was ordered to
open its doors to women. This brought the expected protests about
freedom of association—and of sanctuary. For that has been one of the
points of the men's club. It wasn't open to women. Members knew
women had their place, and everyone knew it was not there. In the
advertisements, as in the world of reality, there is a place for women in
men's lives, one that revolves around:

Sex and Seduction

As suggested earlier, the growing fascination with appearances,
encouraged by advertising, has led to a "feminization" of culture. We
are all put in the classic role of the female: manipulable, submissive,
seeing ourselves as objects. This "feminization of sexuality" is clearly
seen in men's advertisements, where many of the promises made to
women are now made to men. If women's advertisements cry, "Buy
(this product) and he will notice you," men's advertisements similarly
promise that female attention will follow immediately upon purchase,
or shortly thereafter. "They can't stay away from Mr. J." "Master of Art
of Attracting Attention." She says, "He's wearing my favorite Corbin
again." Much as in the advertisements directed at women, the advertisements of men's products promise that they will do the talking for
you. "For the look that says come closer." "All the French you'll ever
need to know."

Although many advertisements show an admiring and/or dependent female, others depict women in a more active role. "I love him—
but life in the fast lane starts at 6 A.M.," says the attractive blonde tying
on her jogging shoes, with the "him" in question very handsome and
very asleep on the bed in the background. (Does this mean he's in the
slow lane?) In another, the man slouches silhouetted against a wall; the
woman leans aggressively toward him. He: "Do you always serve Tia
Maria . . . or am I special?" She: "Darling, if you weren't special . . .
you wouldn't be here."

The masculine role of always being in charge is a tough one. The
blunt new honesty about sexually transmitted diseases such as AIDS
appears in men's magazines as in women's, in the same "I enjoy sex,
but I'm not ready to die for it" condom advertisement. But this new

fear is accompanied by old fears of sexual embarrassment and/or rejection. The cartoon shows a man cringing with embarrassment in a pharmacy as the pharmacist yells out, "Hey, there's a guy here wants some information on Trojans." ("Most men would like to know more about Trojan brand condoms. But they're seriously afraid of suffering a spectacular and terminal attack of embarrassment right in the middle of a well-lighted drugstore.") Compared with such agony and responsibility, advertisements promising that women will *want* whatever is on offer, and will even meet the male halfway, must come as blessed relief. Men can finally relax, leaving the courting to the product and seduction to the beguiled woman, which, surely, must seem nice for a change.

Masculine Homilies

A homily is a short sermon, discourse, or informal lecture, often on a moral topic and suggesting a course of conduct. Some of the most intriguing advertisements offer just that, short statements and bits of advice on what masculinity is and on how real men should conduct themselves. As with many short sermons, many of the advertising homilies have a self-congratulatory air about them; after all, you do not want the consumer to feel bad about himself.

What is it, then, to be a man? It is to be *independent.* "There are some things a man will not relinquish." Among them, says the advertisement, his Tretorn tennis shoes.

It is to *savor freedom.* "Dress easy, get away from it all and let Tom Sawyer paint the fence," advises Alexander Julian, the men's designer. "Because man was meant to fly, we gave him wings"(even if only on his sunglasses).

It is to live a life of *adventure.* KL Homme cologne is "for the man who lives on the edge." Prudential Life Insurance preaches, "If you can dream it, you can do it." New Man sportswear tells the reader, "Life is more adventurous when you feel like a New Man."

It is to *keep one's cool.* "J.B. Scotch. A few individuals know how to keep their heads, even when their necks are on the line."

And it is to stay one step *ahead of the competition.* "Altec Lansing. Hear what others only imagine." Alexander Julian again: "Dress up a bit when you dress down. They'll think you know something they don't."

What is it, then, to be a woman? It is to be *dependent.* "A woman needs a man," reads the copy in the Rigolletto advertisement showing a young man changing a tire for a grateful young woman.

The American cowboy as cultural model was not supposed to care for or about appearances. He was what he was, hard-working, straightforward, and honest. He was authentic. Men who cared "too much" about how they looked did not fit this model; the dandy was effete, a European invention, insufficient in masculinity and not red-blooded enough to be a real American. The other cultural model, imported from England, was the gentleman. A gentleman did care about his appearance, in the proper measure and manifestation, attention to tailoring and to quality, understatement rather than exaggeration.[10]

From the gray flannel suit of the 1950s to the "power look" of the 1980s, clothes made the man fit in with his company's image. Sex appeal and corporate correctness merged in a look that spelled success, that exuded confidence.

Whether or not a man presumed to care about his appearance, he did care about having "the right stuff," as Tom Wolfe and *Esquire* call it, or "men's toys," as in a recent special issue of *M* magazine. Cars, motorcycles, stereos, sports equipment: these are part of the masculine appearance. They allow the man to demonstrate his taste, his special knowledge, his affluence: to extend his control. He can be and is demanding, for only the best will do.

He also wants to be loved, but he does not want to appear needy. Advertisements suggest the magic ability of products ranging from cars to hair creams to attract female attention. With the right products a man can have it all, with no strings attached: no boring marital ties, hefty mortgages, corporate compromises.

According to sociologist Barbara Ehrenreich, *Playboy* magazine did much to legitimate this image of male freedom. The old male ethos, up to the postwar period, required exchanging bachelor irresponsibility for married responsibility, which also symbolized entrance into social adulthood.[11] The perennial bachelor, with his flashy cars and interchangeable women, was the object of both envy and derision; he had fun, but and because he was not fully grown up. There was something frivolous in his lack of purpose and application.

This old ethos has lost much of its legitimacy. Today's male can, as Baudrillard suggests, operate in both modes: the feminine mode of indulging oneself and being indulged and the masculine mode of exigency and competition. With the right look and the right stuff, he can feel confident and manly in boardroom or suburban backyard. Consumer society thus invites both men and women to live in a world of appearances and to devote ever more attention to them.

1. Katz and Katz, *Magazines*, pp. 703–5.

2. Ibid.

3. John Gagnon, "Physical Strength: Once of Significance," in Joseph H. Pleck and Jack Sawyer, eds., *Men and Masculinity* (Englewood Cliffs, N.J.: Prentice-Hall, 1974), pp. 139–49.

4. Baudrillard, *La société de consommation*, pp. 144–47.

5. Ibid.

6. Ibid.

7. Todd Gitlin, "We Build Excitement," in Todd Gitlin, ed., *Watching Television* (New York: Pantheon, 1986), pp.139–40.

8. Ibid.

9. C. Wright Mills, *The Power Elite* (New York: Oxford University Press, 1956), p. 141.

10. See Diane Barthel, "A Gentleman and a Consumer: A Sociological Look at Man at His Best," paper presented at the annual meeting of the Eastern Sociological Society, March 1983, Baltimore.

11. Barbara Ehrenreich, *The Hearts of Men: American Dreams and the Flight from Commitment* (New York: Anchor Books, 1983).

One of Barthel's purposes, stated directly in the first four paragraphs, is to establish that men are not associated with beauty or fashion magazines, but rather with images of power in magazines such as *Playboy* and *Sports Illustrated*. You might also notice from a sentence such as "The very idea of men's beauty magazines may strike one as odd" that Barthel assumes many readers already do not make an association between men and beauty. Add to this assumption her use of terms such as "'real men'" and "red-blooded" and her discussion of what men are "supposed" and "not supposed" to do, and you can begin to determine an implicit purpose: how we define maleness in society is linked to advertising images. Already you have some key ideas about Barthel's intentions to help you sort out the information that follows.

However, as you continue to read, you can see that the next paragraph—paragraph 5—immediately begins to refine and further specify Barthel's overall purposes. The first sentence basically summarizes the content of the preceding paragraphs, and gives added weight to the link between advertisements and the definition of gender roles. The second sentence directly states: "it is important to emphasize how different cultural attitudes . . . shape the gender roles of men and women." Clearly, because the relationship among culture, advertising, and gender roles has now been repeated several times, you can have confidence that establishing this notion is one of Barthel's major purposes in the essay.

Now look at the remainder of the fifth paragraph, where Barthel emphasizes that cultural attitudes and advertisements are changing. Male imagery is being used in ads for women; female imagery is being used in ads for men. Yet the opposition between "Masculine" and "Feminine" still controls how products and consumers are defined. Are these statements also statements of Barthel's purpose in writing the article?

The introductory or topic sentences of the next few paragraphs suggest that the answer to this question is yes. That is, Barthel is beginning to flesh out, define, and provide examples and illustrations of previously stated points. She is beginning to organize her material around her previously stated purposes. Since the first four paragraphs act as a kind of lead into the fifth paragraph and since what follows the fifth paragraph begins to explain its points in more detail, the fifth paragraph is obviously crucial. You may want to read it again and write down, in your own words, a list of interrelated purposes. Your list might resemble the following:

1. Cultural attitudes as seen in advertising shape gender roles— how we see ourselves, how we define ourselves, how we feel we should behave.
2. Attitudes are changing and so ads are beginning to link women with male imagery and men with female imagery.
3. The main definitions in a consumer society are still divided into "Masculine" and "Feminine" camps.

At this stage, if you are at all uncertain about the purposes you have identified, read the author's final, or summary, paragraph to check if any of your choices are restated. In Barthel's last paragraph, all three of these notions are highlighted: change, the mixing of female and male imagery in ads for men especially, and the invitation in consumer society to define ourselves by appearances. You may notice here that the opposition between masculine and feminine seems less important to the author now than the emphasis on appearance. As you go back to read the full article, you may want to look for how this shift occurs.

Finally, as you become more practiced at determining an author's purpose, take a few minutes when you finish reading to consider what implicit or indirect purposes an author may have in mind. In "A Gentleman and a Consumer," Barthel may be warning us of how powerful advertising is, of how difficult it might be to resist gender roles, or even of how manipulative and shallow a consumer culture is. These implicit purposes may help you find interrelationships among texts and may suggest interesting topics for further research and writing.

By applying the strategy of reading for an author's purpose, you will increase the likelihood of understanding and recalling what you read. Purposes are hooks on which you can hang larger chunks of information. They help you understand why an author has chosen to include particular examples and illustrations, and they help you see how a piece of writing is organized.

Best of all, this strategy provides you with a tool for beginning to make critical judgments. You can move beyond a personal sense of what you liked or did not like in a text, what you knew or did not know, or what you agreed or disagreed with to a more informed sense of how readers and writers interact to create meaning. A possible critical response to Barthel's article, based on determining purpose and then considering how well her purposes are achieved, might be as follows:

> Barthel certainly succeeds in convincing me that magazine ads help define gender roles in a consumer society. She is especially good at showing how car ads identify male qualities, such as power, being in control, and being adventurous, with how men should behave and see themselves. These same male symbols can be used to sell to men products formerly associated only with women—clothes and cologne, for example. She shows how the macho American cowboy image has been changed and softened to the image of the successful gentleman, what she calls "the power look" of the 1980s.
>
> Barthel does not give as many examples of how male imagery is beginning to be used in ads directed to women. It would be interesting to see if the same mixing of images occurs in them. However, it is clear that all of us are encouraged by advertising to judge ourselves and others based on appearance.

This is by no means the only critical response a reader might have to Barthel's essay. But by addressing the author's purpose and focusing on the ways that you think she explains and supports that purpose in the article, you should discover that you have much more to say than "I liked this article."

WORD PLAY: BEING SENSITIVE TO LANGUAGE

Both of the critical reading strategies discussed so far—applying context as a guide and reading for an author's purposes—assume that the process of creating meaning lies in an interplay between reader and text. Such an interplay, however, is not possible unless reader and text share a common language, a set of beliefs about what words say. For example, if this text were written in Spanish and you did not understand that language, you would be effectively excluded from the text. The interchange between reader and text, then, like all social interchanges, is rooted in a communal language: what words mean or might suggest is our basic entry to any written text.

If, therefore, as critical readers, we can learn strategies to help us become more conscious of the words authors choose, the connotations of those words, patterns of words, and common figures of speech, we can increase our sensitivity to a text. Word play, which in this case means analyzing a text on the basis of word choice and patterns of language, is crucial not only in the process of creating meaning, but also in detecting shades of meaning, such as an author's tone, biases, or methods of persuasion.

Definitions

In the study of literature, an author's choice of words is called *diction*. In an analysis of diction, it is important to keep three questions in mind:

What does a word mean?
What does it suggest?
Is there a principle of selection or a pattern in the choices an author has made?

The difference between what a word means and what it might suggest is the difference between a word's denotation and connotation. The *denotation* of a word is usually its dictionary meaning, and denotative language is often associated with making statements. However, sometimes a word's denotation is partly dependent on the context of an academic discipline. For example, the word *tragedy* is used in ordinary discourse to refer to any especially sad event, but in a discussion of Shakespeare's plays, the word refers to a specific dramatic form. When reading, you normally need only look in a standard college dictionary to determine a word's common meaning. You should be aware, though, that the reference section in most college libraries also contains dictionaries of psychology, philosophy, economics, the social sciences, and so on, which offer definitions that are specific to the discipline.

The *connotations* of a word are the suggestions and associations triggered by it, and, as a reader, you can often infer an author's tone and biases, or the mood of a piece of fiction, by paying close attention to the suggestiveness of language. For example, a number of words may have essentially the same meaning, or denotation, while differing significantly in the kinds of associations and attitudes they may call forth. In "The Orchard Walls," the narrator speaks about a painful childhood memory she has never managed to forget, "blot out," or exorcise. Although *forget, blot out,* and *exorcise* have similar denotations, they differ significantly in their connotations: *forget* is fairly neutral; *blot out* suggests an intensity of feeling, a yearning that something not just be forgotten, but that it had never happened; and *exorcise* suggests a desire to cleanse the spirit from an evil possession. Similarly, in "A Gentleman and a Consumer," Diane Barthel relies on her readers' abilities to understand the suggestiveness of language in order to analyze the inferences of advertisements. In a slogan such as "Because man was meant to fly, we gave him wings," it is expected that we can make an association between maleness (man) and a spirit of freedom and adventure (flying and wings).

This advertising slogan is also interesting because it is an example of *figurative language.* We are not meant to take this statement literally, that is, to think of a man with actual wings. Instead, we understand that the person who wrote the slogan is using a figure of speech, making an associative link between the wing logo on a pair of sunglasses and the wings of a bird, which allow it to fly. Whereas an author uses literal images to give a reader a sense of specific, concrete, and often sensual detail (how things look, sound, smell, taste, or feel), figurative images allow imaginative connections between dissimilar objects or entities—sunglasses and wings for example.

There are many figures of speech available to an author, but two of the most commonly used are similes and metaphors. A *simile* makes an explicit comparison between two dissimilar objects or entities, using a comparative word such as "like" or "as." If, in writing about "The Orchard Walls," you stated that the young girl thought Ella was as beautiful as a movie queen, you would be using a simile to make a direct comparison between Ella and the appearance, glamour, and perhaps even the remoteness of a movie star.

As the following cartoon illustrates, a *metaphor* is not meant to be taken literally:

THE FAR SIDE

by Gary Larson

"Don't touch it, honey ... it's just a face in the crowd."

Instead, a *metaphor* makes implicit or indirect comparisons, often defining an abstract concept by means of the concrete. In the context of advertising, we might read a sentence like "Good taste is a Ralph Lauren suit." Here, the abstract qualities associated with good taste are given definition by means of a specific article of clothing and a brand name. As Barthel suggests, such a metaphorical slogan would likely also be accompanied by a set of visual images related to good looks, wealth, and success, all of which are meant to become part of our perception of good taste. Single words, too, can be used metaphorically, as in "the car sailed along the highway." Here, the car is given the properties normally associated with a ship gliding smoothly through water.

Because human experience is so rich and language is limited, authors sometimes also use *symbols* to convey a cluster of ideas and feelings that would otherwise be difficult to name. A symbol might be defined as a figure of speech that embodies a concrete image or reality but also suggests an additional level of meaning beyond that reality.

Symbols attempt to make the unknown known, to give physical shape or form to abstract ideas and feelings. A gun might be said to symbolize violence, to embody a complex social pattern of crime and lawlessness. However, symbols seldom have a fixed meaning—guns might also represent law and order or power or authority—so it is important to relate the possible meanings that might be inferred from a symbol to the context in which it is being used. The cherry trees in "The Orchard Walls," for example, symbolize a complex pattern of interrelated ideas—the lush beauty of the countryside, the forbidden fruit of illicit love, and the young girl's fall from innocence. Symbols are an especially rich source of meaning, and a careful reader should allow for a number of possible interpretations.

Figures of speech are often vivid and original, and authors employ them for special effect or emphasis and for communicating complex ideas and feelings that evade literal expression. Sometimes, figures of speech can be used playfully, as in Rachel de Queiroz's story, "Metonymy, or the Husband's Revenge." She spins the entire tale from a fascination with a figure of speech in which a detail is made to represent a whole or a word is used for another word associated with it. By reading the story, you will see how this definition of metonymy is made clear and understandable through a series of dramatic events and concrete details.

The key to effective word play is to appreciate and be open to the flexibility and suggestiveness of language. Although any choice of words may be significant, a pattern of words and images will certainly be so. The guiding question is, "What does language contribute to the meaning of the work as a whole?"

METONOMY, OR THE HUSBAND'S REVENGE

Rachel de Queiroz

Metonymy. I learned the word in 1930 and shall never forget it. I had just published my first novel. A literary critic had scolded me because my hero went out into the night "chest unclosed."

"What deplorable nonsense!" wrote this eminently sensible gentleman. "Why does she not say what she means? Obviously, it was his shirt unclosed, not his chest."

I accepted the rebuke with humility, indeed with shame. But my illustrious Latin professor, Dr. Matos Peixoto, came to my rescue. He said that what I had written was perfectly correct; that I had used a respectable figure of speech known as metonymy; and that this figure consisted in the use of a word for another word associated with it—for example, a word representing a cause instead of the effect, or representing the container when the content is intended. The classic instance, he told me, is "the sparkling cup"; in reality, not the cup but the wine in it is sparkling.

The professor and I wrote a letter which was published in the newspaper where the review had appeared. It put my unjust critic in his place. I hope he learned a lesson. I know I did. Ever since, I have been using metonymy—my only bond with classical rhetoric.

Moreover, I have devoted some thought to it, and I have concluded that metonymy may be more than a figure of speech. There is, I believe, such a thing as practical or applied metonymy. Let me give a crude example, drawn from my own experience. A certain lady of my acquaintance suddenly moved out of the boardinghouse where she had been living for years and became a mortal enemy of the woman who owned it. I asked her why. We both knew that the woman was a kindly soul; she had given my friend injections when she needed them, had often loaned her a hot-water bag, and had always waited on her when she had her little heart attacks. My friend replied:

"It's the telephone in the hall. I hate her for it. Half the time when I answered it, the call was a hoax or joke of some sort."

"But the owner of the boardinghouse didn't perpetrate these hoaxes. She wasn't responsible for them."

"No. But whose telephone was it?"

I know another case of applied metonymy, a more disastrous one for it involved a crime. It happened in a city of the interior, which I shall not name for fear that someone may recognize the parties and revive the scandal. I shall narrate the crime but conceal the criminal.

Well, in this city of the interior there lived a man. He was not old but he was spent, which is worse than being old. In his youth he had suffered from beriberi. His legs were weak, his chest was tired and asthmatic, his skin was yellowish, and his eyes were rheumy. He was, however, a man of property: he owned the house in which he lived and the one next to it, in which he had set up a grocery store. Therefore, although so unattractive personally, he was able to find himself a wife. In all justice to him, he did not tempt fate by marrying a beauty. Instead, he married a poor, emaciated girl, who worked in a men's clothing factory. By her face one would have thought she had consumption. So our friend felt safe. He did not foresee the effects of good nutrition and a healthful life on a woman's appearance. The girl no longer spent eight hours a day at a sewing table. She was the mistress of her house. She ate well: fresh meat, cucumber salad, pork fat with beans and manioc mush, all kinds of sweets, and oranges, which her husband bought by the gross for his customers. The effects were like magic. Her body filled out, especially in the best places. She even seemed to grow taller. And her face—what a change! I may have forgot to mention that her features, in themselves, were good to begin with. Moreover, money enabled her to embellish her natural advantages with art: she began to wear makeup, to wave her hair, and to dress well.

Lovely, attractive, she now found her sickly, prematurely old husband a burden and a bore. Each evening, as soon as the store was closed, he dined, mostly on milk (he could not stomach meat), took his newspaper, and rested on his chaise lounge until time to go to bed. He did not care for the movies or for soccer or for radio. He did not even show much interest in love. Just a sort of tepid, tasteless cohabitation.

And then Fate intervened: it produced a sergeant.

Granted, it was unjust for a young wife, after being reconditioned at her husband's expense, to employ her charms to the prejudice of the aforesaid husband. Unjust; but, then, this world thrives on injustice, doesn't it? The sergeant—I shall not say whether he was in the Army, the Air Force, the Marines, or the Fusileers, for I still mean to conceal the identities of the parties—the sergeant was muscular, young, ingratiating, with a manly, commanding voice and a healthy spring in his walk. He looked gloriously martial in his high-buttoned uniform.

One day, when the lady was in charge of the counter (while her husband lunched), the sergeant came in. Exactly what happened and what did not happen, is hard to say. It seems that the sergeant asked for a pack of cigarettes. Then he wanted a little vermouth. Finally, he asked permission to listen to the sports broadcast on the radio next to the counter. Maybe it was just an excuse to remain there awhile. In any case, the girl said it would be all right. It is hard to refuse a favor to a sergeant, especially a sergeant like this one. It appears that the sergeant asked nothing more that day. At most, he and the girl exchanged expressive glances and a few agreeable words, murmured so softly that the customers, always alert for something to gossip about, could not hear them.

Three times more the husband lunched while his wife chatted with the sergeant in the store. The flirtation progressed. Then the husband fell ill with a grippe, and the two others went far beyond flirtation. How and when they met, no one was able to discover. The important thing is that they were lovers and that they loved with a forbidden love, like Tristan and Isolde or Paolo and Francesca.

Then Fate, which does not like illicit love and generally punishes those who engage in it, transferred the sergeant to another part of the country.

It is said that only those who love can really know the pain of separation. The girl cried so much that her eyes grew red and swollen. She lost her appetite. Beneath her rouge could be seen the consumptive complexion of earlier times. And these symptoms aroused her husband's suspicion, although, curiously, he had never suspected anything when the love affair was flourishing and everything was wine and roses.

He began to observe her carefully. He scrutinized her in her periods of silence. He listened to her sighs and to the things she murmured in her sleep. He snooped around and found a postcard and book, both with a man's name in the same handwriting. He found the insignia of the sergeant's regiment and concluded that the object of his wife's murmurs, sighs, and silences was not only a man but a soldier. Finally he made the supreme discovery: that they had indeed betrayed him. For he discovered the love letters, bearing airmail stamps, a distant postmark, and the sergeant's name. They left no reasonable doubt.

For five months the poor fellow twisted the poisoned dagger of jealousy in his thin, sickly chest. Like a boy who discovers a birds' nest and, hiding nearby, watches the eggs increasing in number every day, so the husband, using a duplicate key to the wood chest where his wife put her valuables, watched the increase in the number of letters concealed there. He had given her the chest during their honeymoon, saying, "Keep your secrets here." And the ungrateful girl had obeyed him.

Every day at the fateful hours of lunch, she replaced her husband at the counter. But he was not interested in eating. He ran to her room, pulled out a drawer of her bureau, removed the chest from under a lot of panties, slips, and such, took the little key out of his pocket, opened the chest, and anxiously read the new letter. If there was no new letter, he reread the one dated August 21st; it was so full of realism that it sounded like dialogue from a French movie. Then he put everything away and hurried to the kitchen, where he swallowed a few spoonfuls of broth and gnawed at a piece of bread. It was almost impossible to swallow with the passion of those two thieves sticking in his throat.

When the poor man's heart had become utterly saturated with jealousy and hatred, he took a revolver and a box of bullets from the counter drawer; they had been left, years before, by a customer as security for a debt, which had never been paid. He loaded the revolver.

One bright morning at exactly ten o'clock, when the store was full of customers, he excused himself and went through the doorway that connected the store with his home. In a few seconds the customers heard the noise of a row, a woman's scream, and three shots. On the sidewalk in front of the shopkeeper's house they saw his wife on her knees, still screaming, and him, with the revolver in his trembling hand, trying to raise her. The front door of the house was open. Through it, they saw a man's legs, wearing khaki trousers and boots. He was lying face down, with his head and torso in the parlor, not visible from the street.

The husband was the first to speak. Raising his eyes from his wife, he looked at the terror-stricken people and spotted among them his favorite customer. He took a few steps, stood in the doorway, and said:

"You may call the police."

At the police station he explained that he was a deceived husband. The police chief remarked:

"Isn't this a little unusual? Ordinarily you kill your wives. They're weaker than their lovers."

The man was deeply offended.

"No," he protested, "I would be utterly incapable of killing my wife. She is all that I have in the world. She is refined, pretty, and hard-working. She helps me in the store, she understands bookkeeping, she writes the letters to the wholesalers. She is the only person who knows how to prepare my food; I have a special diet. Why should I want to kill my wife?"

"I see," said the chief of police. "So you killed her lover."

The man shook his head.

"Wrong again. The sergeant—her lover—was transferred to a place far away from here. I discovered the affair only after he had gone. By reading his letters. They tell the whole story. I know one of them by heart, the worst of them. . . ."

The police chief did not understand. He said nothing and waited for the husband to continue, which he presently did:

"Those letters! If they were alive I would kill them, one by one. They were shameful to read—almost like a book. I thought of taking an airplane trip. I thought of killing some other sergeant here, so that they would all learn a lesson not to fool around with another man's wife. But I was afraid of the rest of the regiment; you know how these military men stick together. Still, I had to do something. Otherwise I would have gone crazy. I couldn't get those letters out of my head. Even on days when none arrived I felt terrible, worse than my wife. I had to put an end to it, didn't I? So today, at last I did it. I waited till the regular time and, when I saw the wretch appear on the other side of the street, I went into the house, hid behind a door, and lay there for him." "The lover?" asked the police chief stupidly.

"No, of course not. I told you that I didn't kill her lover. It was those letters. The sergeant sent them—but *he* delivered them. Almost every day, there he was at the door, smiling, with the vile envelope in his hand. I pointed the revolver and fired three times. He didn't say a word; he just fell. No, chief, it wasn't her lover. It was the mailman."

Translated from the Portuguese by William L. Grossman.

Strategies for Word Play

In order to help sensitize you to the importance of language in constructing the meaning of a text, here are three specific critical reading strategies you can begin to apply:

Reading for repetition
Reading for patterns of words and images
Reading the title as a code

These three strategies, used singly or in combination, will help you become more aware of an author's craft. The information you gather from applying them can also be used as textual evidence to support your particular view of a text's overall meaning.

Illustration

Reading for Repetition

In this strategy, you simply list words or ideas repeated by an author. Repetition is used for emphasis, so when authors repeat certain words or images, they are signaling their importance to the reader. It is then up to the reader to infer or determine the significance of the repeated words.

As you read "A Gentleman and a Consumer," you may have noted that Barthel persistently repeats words and phrases linked to masculinity:

real man
male imagery
masculine models
masculine competition
male role
men's advertisements
male markets
masculine symbols, language, and imagery
manly model
masculine homilies
masculine appearance
masculine mode

This list leaves no doubt about the subject of the article; however, if you group the list into categories, you might also gain some insight into how Barthel constructs her argument.

Masculine Role	→	Advertising	→	Tools of Advertising
↓		↓		↓
real man		men's advertisements		male imagery
male role		male markets		masculine symbols

Here, words having to do with the masculine role itself are separated from words associated first with advertising and then with how advertising communicates. Now you can infer that masculinity is defined in advertising by means of male symbols and imagery. You can practice reading for repetition by seeing if there is repetition in the kinds of advertisements Barthel includes or repetition in the male imagery they use.

Reading for Patterns of Words and Images

Suppose, that as you read "The Orchard Walls" you notice Rendell's repetition of the images of cherries and cherry trees but are unsure of the significance of this repetition. Listing or underlining all of the descriptive words, feelings, and events connected with the cherries may help you discover a pattern of meaning. You would be reading not just for the repetition of the same or similar words, but for a cluster of ideas, connotations, and descriptions that may revolve around this single image.

Now try to discover patterns in these descriptions and events by grouping together like qualities. On the one hand, the cherries clearly evoke painful memories—the narrator "winces" when she sees them and refers to cherry pie as part of "a devil's menu." The cherry trees outside Ella's bedroom window are crucial to the advancement of the plot and to the central crime. They play a significant role in the narrator's disgrace when she mistakes a scarecrow in the trees for a dead body. The connotations of these words and events are negative.

On the other hand, the cherries are also associated with the beauty of the farm, with adventure, and with romance. The girl, whose romantic fantasies have been stressed in the story, imagines Ella climbing down a cherry tree from her bedroom to meet her lover and, thus, easily imagines (and, ironically, imagines correctly) Dennis being shot in the same tree, for the same reason. As the details of the story unfold, there is a parallel between the blossoming love affair and the ripening fruit—the cherries begin to turn color, "with a blush coming to their cheeks." The sensual connotations of words describing the fruit seem connected to the developing theme of sexuality.

Finally, the cherries are linked to a loss of innocence and a fall from grace: the cherry festival belongs to a time of innocence before the war; and the girl eats a cherry immediately before blurting out her mistaken discovery explicitly linked to murder and adultery. By focusing on the words and images related to the cherry trees, it is possible to see that they function both in a literal and figurative way, giving concrete and sensual detail to the narrative, but also suggesting deeper and symbolic levels of meaning.

A much simpler illustration of how reading for patterns of words and images can help you infer meaning can be drawn from Rachel de Queiroz's story. Consider the chain of words used to describe the husband:

old
spent
weak
tired
asthmatic
a burden
a bore
a man of property

Here is the chain of words used to describe the sergeant:

muscular
young
ingratiating
manly
commanding
healthy

The sum of these parts is inevitable. To use a metaphorical expression, "the writing is on the wall" because of this clear, and even humorous, contrast. That the husband is later described as suspicious, scrutinizing, snoopy, and obsessed with jealousy is no surprise to the reader. Although this story, like Rendell's, tells a tale of murder and adultery, the tone is much different, partly because of word choice and unambiguous, familiar patterns of opposition.

Reading the Title as Code

This strategy is especially easy to apply and assumes that, more often than not, an author or editor will choose a title to encode meaning, to provide hints to the reader about purpose, content, tone, or theme. Thus, keeping a title in mind as you read can often help you identify significant passages or images or help you categorize information. At first, Rendell's title does not seem to provide any clues as to what her story may be about, but it soon becomes very significant, directing the reader to the quote from *Romeo and Juliet* and emphasizing the themes of forbidden love, danger, and family honor.

Since metonymy is not a common word, Rachel de Queiroz's title, "Metonymy, or the Husband's Revenge," may initially puzzle a reader. However, it quickly becomes clear that much of the story illustrates the term. Thus, the title encodes one of the author's purposes in writing and even hints at its lighthearted tone. While reading the story, you might also detect the ways in which the author suggests how the power of language (letters and fiction) can shape human experience— a possible meaning that the title, in linking a figure of speech with a human act, also supports.

Barthel's title, "A Gentleman and a Consumer," directs the reader's attention to how gentlemen and consumers are described. She stresses that the currently dominant image of the gentleman is different from the traditional American cowboy—less macho, more concerned with appearance, but still manly. Consumers, we learn as we read, are feminized, that is, associated with submission (buy this product), conscious of how they are judged by appearances, and easily manipulated (buy this product instead of that one). Thus, Barthel's title can be seen as a kind of shorthand, summarizing some of the key elements of her argument: both male and female imagery is being used in advertisements to define identity based on appearances.

Critical readers use these three strategies to analyze both fiction and nonfiction. The more you practice them, the more automatic they will become in the process of creating meaning. This kind of textual analysis will also be invaluable if you are asked to write about a text, giving supporting reasons for your interpretations. There should always be some connection between the meaning you have constructed and word choice, patterns of words and images, or titles.

DIALOGUING WITH A TEXT: ACHIEVING BALANCE

The interplay that occurs between reader and text in the process of creating meaning might be described as a conversation or dialogue. As you know from your own experience, dialogues are not always balanced: sometimes one speaker dominates the conversation at the expense of the other. A similar imbalance may occur in the reading process. If the reader is too passive, not involved in the text, or overwhelmed by the text's complexity, the reading process becomes dominated by the text. However, if the reader is not open-minded or disregards the features of a text, then the reading process becomes dominated by the reader. In either case, the effort to construct a meaningful whole from the elements of a text will be hindered.

An effective critical reader strives to achieve a balanced dialogue with a text in order to maximize the potential for comprehension and learning. Attaining this balance requires both a sense of involvement and empathy with a text and a measure of detachment, which allows for critical evaluation and judgment.

In practice, though, how can readers check for this balance and develop confidence in their ability to carry on an effective dialogue with a text? Two of the most helpful strategies are to write about a text and to construct a mental map of a text. Both of these techniques require readers to be active and analytical, that is, to translate the text into personally meaningful terms, to note ways in which the text is organized, and to consider how a text relates to past experience or prior knowledge. Unlike description, which summarizes plot or repeats textual information, analysis requires a reader to make relationships among the features of a text, and to synthesize these parts into a meaningful whole. The more you practice writing about or mapping a text, the more skilled you will become at checking for a balanced approach, reading critically, and thinking analytically.

Writing About a Text

Many college courses require students to keep journals or reading logs in order to encourage writing about a text. There are several significant advantages to this strategy. Writing is a powerful tool for learning; therefore, keeping a written record of the responses you have to a text while you read it or immediately afterward not only helps you focus on your role as reader in creating meaning, but also demands that you manipulate the text in an active way. *Manipulating* a text, in this context, simply means that in writing your responses you are encoding your own impressions, and the possible meanings you can assign to a text, as well as highlighting some of its dominant features. When you manipulate a machine, you are actually using it and learning about it in an active and practical way, and the same is true of manipulating a text.

Furthermore, the act of writing requires a level of engagement much more intense than merely underlining or highlighting what you consider to be the significant points in a text. By writing, you are likely to find and create relationships among ideas, and to connect new information to prior knowledge; as a result, you will be better able to recall information. Finally, a written record of your responses to what you have read also allows you to track your development as a critical reader: the more you employ this strategy, the sharper your skills will become. As you gain more confidence, you can reread earlier responses and make revisions or simply notice emerging patterns in your own reading process.

For all these reasons, you should practice dialogue with a text by writing about it, even if journals or reading logs are not assigned in a course. To begin, you need to set up some guidelines for your reading responses:

1. Focus on what you are thinking, feeling, and responding to as you read, rather than on a polished style. This is writing you do for yourself, so it can be informal.
2. To practice analysis and move beyond description, direct part of

your response to issues of context, purpose, or language, all of which can help you assign meanings to a text.

3. Ask yourself critical questions about the traditionally significant parts of a text, such as introductions and conclusions. What kinds of expectations does the introduction raise, for example? Is the author's purpose (or purposes) clear? How does the conclusion contribute to the overall meaning of the text?

4. Keep in mind questions that will help you link what you are reading to past or prior knowledge, questions that will help you check for both involvement with and critical distance from the text, such as "What associations can I make to past experience?" and "In what ways does the text help me restructure past experience or rethink an issue?"

5. Try to make some connections between the reading you have been assigned and the course of study you are taking. How does a specific reading relate to the theory or concepts of the course as a whole?

Illustration

Here is one experienced reader's response to Rachel de Queiroz's short story "Metonymy, or the Husband's Revenge." In reading it, remember that your own response is likely to be quite different, but equally valid. This response is offered only as a guide as to how you might write about your own ideas and feelings in an analytical way:

> I found myself wanting to read this story because of the title—it reminds me of a riddle. I had no idea what metonymy meant but was curious about what it might have to do with a husband's revenge. The author wastes no time in explaining the key word, but her stories about "applied" metonymy are much more fun than a dictionary definition of a figure of speech. Even though the introductory section and the little story about the woman who hated the telephone should have warned me what to expect, I was still surprised when the husband shot the postman. He hates the letters his wife gets from her lover, so he kills the mailman. The post (the letters and who delivers them) is an example of metonymy.
>
> Why does a story about a murder strike me as funny? Part of the reason is that it is not told from a moral point of

view, but as an illustration of a term. Another reason may be the surprise I felt—the ending solves the riddle or is like the punch line of a joke. So the story line or sequence of events seems more important to me when reading than the characters or their motivations.

We have been talking in class about different kinds of narratives and purposes a writer might have. I think what I learned from reading this story is how creative a writer might be in defining or illustrating a term. Using a story to explain a concept makes a lot of sense to me.

There is one question still bothering me, though. It's the term "applied" metonymy, which seems to be about acting out a figure of speech. I'm not sure what the implication of this is—maybe it has to do with the power of language to shape our lives?

Again, although your particular response to the story might be quite different, note how this experienced reader is allowing personal expectations and past experiences to shape the meaning of the text. The reader cites the idea of a riddle, feelings of surprise, and expected reactions to a murder to help build a response based on a dialogue with the text. The reader is involved with the story but still able to be objective about how it achieves its goals.

The reader also uses context and an awareness of an author's purpose as reading strategies, making links between the story and the field of study or course in which it has been assigned. Furthermore, by assigning meaning and noting the importance of the story's beginning and ending, this response is analytical rather than descriptive, although not all of the reader's questions are resolved. Clearly, the reader here is interacting with the text and not merely repeating its plot.

Mapping a Text

Mapping the key features of a text is a particularly effective strategy for reading nonfiction. To construct a mental map of an essay or article, you must identify for yourself the terms and images that best encapsulate the meaning you have assigned to the text. Your mental map, then, provides an overview of the essay, highlighting the main features that can later prompt you to reconstruct meaning and recall larger chunks of information. You can use words, phrases, headings, visual prompts or graphics, or some combination of these tools to map a text, but your resulting mental map should be short and simple. If your map becomes too long or complex, you run the risk of merely recording or copying textual information or of getting lost in the trees (textual details) at the expense of the forest (overview of text). Mental maps, like writing about a text, require you to manipulate textual features actively and, in so doing, practice analysis.

Illustration

Suppose that after reading Barthel's "A Gentleman and a Consumer" you decide that her main point is as follows: the shift in recent advertisements directed at men proves that gender roles and identity are increasingly based on appearances. The mental map you construct to encode this meaning might look like this:

The Marlboro Man

↓

Gentlemen Prefer Blondes

↑

The Blondes

Key Terms: masculine and feminine imagery

the feminization of the consumer

symbols of status and success—
"the right look, the right stuff"

emphasis on male appearance

Here the meaning is encoded by means of popular advertising slogans or identities (Gentlemen Prefer Blondes) based solely on appearance: the rugged cowboy is translated into the more sophisticated gentleman who makes choices. The gentleman consumer, as the arrows indicate, combines traits of both the manly cowboy and the blondes defined solely by their appearance. The accompanying list of key terms triggers for the reader important arguments or evidence in support of this meaning.

You can also make a different mental map, one that charts organization and makes use of the essay's subtitles:

Advertisements

Masculine	*Feminine*
Power, performance, precision	Passive, narcissistic, sexy
↓	↓
Car ads	Beauty products

Avoiding the Feminine

Beauty products are sold to men only by means
of manly names and masculine images.

↓

Sex and Seduction

Men can be sexy and vulnerable too; sometimes
women can be the seducer rather than the seduced.

↓

Masculine Homilies

Ads tell us what masculinity is and how real men
should behave and look.

↓

The right look and the right stuff define who we are—

↓

consumers in a world of appearances.

In this example, note how the main points build to a conclusion. Remember that it does not matter what particular form your mental map takes—you decide what best encodes the meaning you have assigned to a text. However, by applying this strategy, you will be training yourself to read for patterns of meaning and relationships among ideas. Best of all, you will sharpen your analytical skills.

Even though these strategies may seem a little awkward to you at first, they can help you assess your dialogue with a text. If your written responses only retell the story or focus only on your past experiences, or if you are unable to decide upon main points when mapping a text, you need to read the text again. Ask yourself if you are being open-minded enough and, if not, why not? Think about or review the different strategies you can apply before and during the reading process. By being consciously aware of the need for both involvement and detachment, you will improve your chances of understanding and learning.

READING STRATEGY SHEETS FOR FICTION AND NONFICTION

Reading strategy sheets provide a very structured method for undertaking a dialogue with a text. Unlike informal written responses and mapping strategies, which usually follow reading and allow the reader considerable freedom in terms of focus, reading strategy sheets make explicit the kinds of recurring questions critical readers ask themselves while they read and construct meaning. In other words, strategy sheets are a way of structuring the reading process itself. As you use them, you will be practicing your skills as a reader, and gradually you will internalize the kinds of questions that need to be asked in building toward a critical response to the text. The specific questions provided by the strategy sheets will guide you through a text, prompting you to think about and respond to important categories and textual features. In a sense, the strategy sheets will interrupt your natural tendency to focus solely on the story line or the factual content and cause you to take note of how a reader and text interact to create patterns of meaning.

Because reading strategy sheets slow down the reading process and encourage very detailed responses you may choose to use them selectively. Rather than attempting to fill them out for every text you are asked to read, you may want to save them for the following situations:

1. To practice your critical reading skills at the beginning of a course, and then once or twice each term
2. To cope with a very difficult text
3. To take very detailed notes when you are asked to write a formal essay based on a particular text

Reading Strategy Sheets for Fiction

To some extent, the explicit questions chosen here to create a sample reading strategy sheet for short stories and novels summarize specific reading strategies discussed earlier in this book. Using the strategy sheet does not preclude using these other strategies, or vice versa. In fact, the key to becoming an expert reader is to learn a number of strategies and then be able to choose among them for any given text.

The design of reading strategy sheets should be flexible. The questions chosen here are not the only ones that may be raised, although they are typical of the questions readers ask themselves about fiction. You may want to incorporate questions of your own that often occur to you as you read. For instance,

"Would I recommend this novel to a friend?"
"Why, or why not?"
"What most surprised me about this novel?"

You could also talk to some of your classmates about the kinds of questions they ask when reading, and then add to your strategy sheet whatever suggestions seem most useful to you. Finally, you will need to match some of your questions to specific course themes or to the field of study in which you are reading.

The following example of a reading strategy sheet for novels and short stories in a women's studies course or a course dealing with gender issues can serve as a guide:

READING STRATEGY SHEET

Course Title: Images of Women in Popular Fiction

1. Title

What kinds of associations are triggered in your mind by this title? Do you have any guesses or predictions as to what the story or novel is about?

2. Author's Name

Have you read any other books or stories by this author? What background information or context notes do you have that might indicate particular content matter or characteristic style?

3. Copyright Date and Place of Publication

What do you know about the time period when this novel or story was first published and about the culture where it first appeared?

4. Opening Paragraphs or Novel's First Chapter

What are your impressions of the story's opening or of the novel's introductory chapter? What have you learned so far, and what do you think might happen?

5. Character Checklist

Begin listing the names of important characters and the page numbers where they first appear. Also jot down your initial impressions of the character. You can add to this information and note any changes in characters as you continue to read.

6. Points Worth Noting as You Read

The following questions and categories may be useful in helping you respond to the text. Not all will be relevant, but fill in as many as you can. Don't forget page numbers.

a. **Point of View.** Who is telling the story? Is it a character narrator or an omniscient narrator? Does the narrative point of view change during the story or novel?

b. **Figurative Language.** Are there recurring symbols or patterns of imagery? What do you think they contribute to the overall meaning of the story or novel?

c. **Setting and Atmosphere.** What is the setting or mood of the story or novel? How do you respond to details of setting and mood?

d. **Turning Points.** What do you think are the crucial points of action in the plot? Are there important choices made by the characters? Important insights or reactions? Do any of the main characters change?

e. **Style.** Are there any noteworthy patterns in the author's choice of words? Are the sentences short or long, simple or complex? Does the author use dialogue effectively?

f. **Thematic Concerns.** Themes in fiction are usually expressed through a combination of characters, images, and action. Looking for themes is a way of deciding what you think the story or novel may be about. What do you think the various themes of this story or novel might be? List at least two possibilities.

7. The Conclusion

Are you satisfied as a reader by the ending? Is the ending open to more than one interpretation?

8. Overall Impressions and Course Context

What does this story or novel contribute to your knowledge of women's issues and how women and men are viewed by the particular culture?

What assumptions do you think the author makes about women, gender roles, and identity?

How do this author's views of gender compare with the views of other authors you have read in the course or outside of it?

What assumptions of your own were challenged by this story or novel?

Most of the questions on this strategy sheet are general, designed to direct you to some standard features of fictional texts. When working with a particular story or novel, however, you will likely discover that not all the questions are equally relevant in the construction of meaning. For example, the narrative point of view in Ruth Rendell's "The Orchard Walls" is a very noteworthy feature: the story is told from the point of view of an adult recalling crucial events from her adolescence. As a character narrator directly involved in the story's action, the adult only learns the full significance of past events many years later when she reads an article in a newspaper. From the beginning, the reader knows that the newspaper is crucial to the character narrator's view of events, but does not know what the newspaper reveals until the very end. This manner of telling the story is important to its element of suspense and to the themes of innocence, memory, and ill-starred romance. To appreciate how significant the narrative point of view is in shaping a reader's response, you need only imagine how different the story would be if told from the point of view of the murderer.

An author's style—the choice of words, sentence patterns, dialogue, and so on—can also shape a reader's response. Rachel de Queiroz's account of murder in "Metonymy, or the Husband's Revenge" is straightforward and seemingly factual. Her style seems journalistic, revealing "facts" or events in simple, relatively short sentences. This objective style, together with the fact that the characters are only briefly sketched and the narrator is omniscient (all-knowing and standing beyond or outside the events of the story), influences the reader's possible range of responses. It makes more probable a sense of emotional distance from the murder and an acceptance of it as a dramatic, even humorous, illustration of a term.

Once you have filled out your strategy sheet, it should be easier for you to recognize patterns and relationships among the parts of a story or novel. Although you will have to tailor the questions about course context in item 8 on the sheet to the particular course you are taking or to particular course themes, your answers to these questions will help you understand the relationships among a number of stories or the relationships between an assigned reading and the larger issues raised by the course as a whole.

Reading Strategy Sheets for Nonfiction

Most reading strategies can be applied with equal validity to both fiction and nonfiction. However, since the major characteristics of form in essays, articles, and textbooks differ from those in fiction, you will need to rephrase some of the questions you ask yourself when reading nonfiction.

Furthermore, you can carry on a dialogue with nonfiction more effectively by taking note of its typical organizational features. Introductory paragraphs or chapters usually provide an overview of material and a major statement of purpose, sometimes called a thesis statement. The first sentences of paragraphs, called topic sentences, usually contain the main idea of the paragraph. Knowing this, you can begin to separate major points from more specific information, or argument from evidence.

Finally, you should take careful note of any subheadings, illustrations such as graphs or maps, and italicized words and terms. Authors employ these devices to organize larger chunks of material and to emphasize key points. Single words or transition phrases are also used to structure material and can signal that certain kinds of information are likely to follow. Here is a short list of such words and phrases and the expectations they generally raise in a reader. You may want to add to this list as you gain more experience in recognizing the kinds of verbal signposts authors frequently use.

Signpost Words and Phrases

However **Although**	Expect the author to qualify an earlier statement or argument.
On the other hand **In contrast**	Expect the author to provide an opposing view to an earlier statement or argument.
For instance **For example** **To illustrate** **In this case**	Expect the author to provide examples, illustrations, or specific information in support of a main idea or argument.
Significantly **Most importantly**	The author is emphasizing a key statement or piece of information.
To begin **Initially** **First of all** **Before proceeding** **Finally**	The author is signaling major turning points in the text—what is to come, what will be explained, a time to pause, or what has been said.

In designing a reading strategy sheet for nonfiction, then, you will want to repeat some of the pertinent questions used for fiction, but also add some categories tailored to the form and organization of nonfiction. Once again, be sure to include overview and course context questions, for they will help you ground a specific text in the larger issues of the field or theme you are studying. Here is a sample reading strategy sheet for a course on media and mass communication that you can use as a guide.

————————— **READING STRATEGY SHEET** —————————

Course Title: Understanding Media and Mass Communication

1. Title

What kinds of associations are triggered in your mind by this title? Do you have any guesses or predictions as to what the article or book might be about?

2. Author's Name

Have you read any other text by this author? What background information or context notes do you have that might indicate particular content matter or the author's ideological perspective?

3. Copyright Date and Place of Publication

What do you know about the time period when this article or book was first published and about the culture where it first appeared?

4. List of Subtitles or Table of Contents

What kinds of subtopics does the author list as central to the text? Are there any headings that strike you as unusual? Any missing that you expected to find?

5. Opening Paragraphs or Introductory Chapter

What do you think the author's main thesis or controlling argument is? List what you consider to be the stated or implied purposes of the article or book.

6. Points Worth Noting as You Read

The following questions and categories may be useful in helping you respond to the text. Not all will be relevant, but fill in as many as you can. Don't forget page numbers.

a. **Key Terms and Definitions.** Does the author use italics to stress certain terms? Are definitions clear? Jot down in your own words what you think the author's definitions are. Do the textual definitions match, challenge, or expand your own?

b. **Maps, Graphs, and Illustrations.** If the author uses any visual aids, how do these relate to the main thesis or argument?

c. **Quotations and Citations.** Does the author quote or cite the opinions or published work of experts or other authors? How do these references relate to the main thesis or argument?

d. **Examples and Evidence.** Does the author clarify abstract ideas by providing concrete examples? Can you illustrate one of the author's ideas with an example of your own? Is the evidence marshaled in support of the main points convincing? Can you think of any evidence from your own experience or background knowledge that has been excluded by the author?

e. **Assumptions and Biases.** Does the author make any statements that cannot be substantiated or that assume a position that isn't necessarily so? Does the author confess to or otherwise reveal any bias that may be shaping the argument?

f. **Figurative Language.** Are there recurring symbols or patterns of imagery used by the author to reinforce the main points?

g. **Style.** Are there any noteworthy patterns in the author's choice of words? Are the sentences short or long, simple or complex?

7. Concluding Paragraphs or Summary Chapter

Does the author's conclusion restate the main thesis? Are you satisfied as a reader that the main argument has been well supported? Does the author indicate in the closing remarks any related ideas or applications of argument that might be explored further?

8. Overall Impressions and Course Context

What does this article or book contribute to your understanding of media and mass communication?

How do this author's views compare with the views of other authors you have read in the course or outside of it?

What assumptions do you think this author makes about media and mass communication?

What assumptions of your own were challenged by this article or book?

As mentioned earlier, these general questions are intended simply to guide you in structuring the reading process and your dialogue with a text. You and your classmates may think of other questions to add, especially questions frequently posed by your instructor in class discussions or lectures.

You should remember, too, that the main advantage of using strategy sheets lies in mastering the questioning technique itself. As you practice this strategy, you will be learning what to look for in a text and what to think about while reading. Feel free to use the sheets flexibly— you can skip ahead to certain questions or go back to others as you read. Since each reader brings his or her own knowledge and purpose for reading to a text, there will be a wide range of valid responses. In filling out the strategy sheets, you should not be pressured by searching for "right" answers. Rather, the material you collect will help you make your own decisions about what the text is saying and how it may contribute to your process of learning.

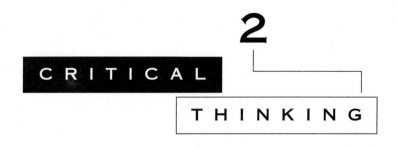

CRITICAL
2
THINKING

PROBLEM SOLVING: VERTICAL AND LATERAL THINKING

Thinking is a complex activity that we engage in whenever we question, analyze, or try to make sense of a situation, a set of behaviors, or a piece of information. We think to solve a wide variety of problems, to relate what we are learning to what we know, and to communicate what we think we know to others in an organized and persuasive way. Critical thinking might be defined, then, as becoming aware of something you already do—becoming conscious of your own thinking process and that of others.

Still, how do we think? We have all been told at some time in our lives that we are not thinking or that we are not thinking hard enough or that we are not thinking clearly. The somewhat mysterious process of thinking, and especially of thinking critically, becomes demystified if we can identify and name specific activities that we engage in when we are thinking. These activities might include asking pertinent questions, trying to view a situation from a variety of perspectives, trying to generate alternatives, testing or weighing evidence, and being open to new ideas. Once you begin to isolate some of the activities involved in thinking, you will find it easier to learn strategies that promote more effective thinking.

Critical thinking encourages you to examine carefully the steps you follow and the activities you engage in when you think. Critical thinking is also developmental—that is, by becoming aware of what you do or might not do when you think, you can learn and practice skills that will improve your thinking. Finally, critical thinking is active. It demands that you use your initiative and develop your sense of curiosity, that you become involved enough to grapple with issues and tackle problems, and that you try to think for yourself and not just rely on the thinking of others.

Perhaps the first step in becoming a critical thinker is to recognize that effective thinking involves both a logical, sequential frame of mind and a creative, generative one. Edward de Bono, an expert on thinking, resolves this apparent contradiction by identifying two kinds of thinking: vertical and lateral. He also stresses that we need both kinds of thinking in order to minimize errors and cope with a variety of situations.[1]

Vertical thinking is the kind of thinking we are most familiar with, often calling it logical or traditional thinking. It follows a sequential pattern, working step by step toward the best solution to a problem. Vertical thinking is concerned with rightness and, to proceed successfully, we need to ensure that each step on the path to a solution is correct. Thus, vertical thinking requires us to make judgments, to determine whether a step is right or wrong, as we follow the most likely path toward a solution.

In contrast, lateral thinking is associated with humor, insight, and creativity. It follows the least likely paths, and is often provocative. Lateral thinking challenges accepted patterns and definitions, and so encourages us to suspend judgments. It is exploring and speculative, inviting us to generate ideas and experiment with different approaches to a situation.

As de Bono insists, we need to be aware of both kinds of thinking in order to function effectively. Though they have different characteristics, vertical and lateral thinking are partners rather than antagonists. A person who engaged only in lateral thinking might generate lots of new ideas but would lack the skills to develop them. A person who engaged only in vertical thinking might find a solution to a problem but never imagine that there could be a better solution or a faster way of arriving at it.

Close-ended Problems

To experience for yourself the different uses of vertical and lateral thinking, you need to apply your thinking skills to different kinds of problems. To begin, try to solve the logic puzzle that follows. It is an example of a close-ended problem, or a problem that has one correct answer.

1. Edward de Bono *Lateral Thinking* (London: Penguin Books, 1990) 7–13.

| LOGIC PUZZLE

Mary calls her friends to arrange a summer picnic in the park. Each of the four couples attending agrees to contribute a different item to the menu. One boy's name is Peter, and each couple consists of one girl and one boy. From the following clues, can you determine the names of each couple, and the item each couple brings? One couple brings sodas.

1. Joanne, Billy, and Dan each bring something different. None of them brings hot dogs.
2. Sue doesn't bring the green salad.
3. Joanne doesn't bring the potato salad.
4. Sam, who doesn't bring the green salad, has never met Kate.
5. Sue, who doesn't know Dan, doesn't bring hot dogs.
6. Billy doesn't bring the potato salad.

The clues contain enough information for you to solve the puzzle correctly, but you will need a chart to help you record all the information. The following table will help you get started; it records the information from the first clue.

Girl's Name:	Joanne			
Boy's Name:		Billy	Dan	
Item:				hot dogs

Before reading the full solution, grapple with the puzzle yourself, and try to fill in the blanks remaining in the chart.

Solution

Each couple brings only one item, and the hot dogs can only be brought by either Peter or Sam (clue 1). Since Sue doesn't bring the hot dogs either and doesn't know Dan (clue 5), she must come with Billy. Since Sue doesn't bring the green salad (clue 2) and Billy doesn't bring the potato salad (clue 6), they must be the couple who brings the sodas. Joanne doesn't bring the potato salad (clue 3) or the hot dogs (clue 1), so, by process of elimination, she must bring the green salad. Sam doesn't bring the green salad (clue 4), so, by elimination, Joanne must come with Peter. Sam has never met Kate (clue 4), so he can only come with Mary. Therefore, Kate must come with Dan. They cannot bring the hot dogs (clue 1), so the only item left for them to bring is the potato salad. In summary, here are the names of each couple and the item each brings to the picnic:

> Joanne and Peter bring the green salad.
> Sue and Billy bring the sodas.
> Kate and Dan bring the potato salad.
> Mary and Sam bring the hot dogs.

Logic puzzles like this one can be solved by using only vertical thinking skills. Each conclusion must be correct to proceed, and the puzzle is solved by following one pathway of logic. You will find the correct matches by following a process of elimination. Logic puzzles also provide all the necessary information for arriving at a solution, and, since the problem is close-ended, the answer that fits in with all the clues must be the right answer. However, effective critical thinkers need to be able to cope with a range of problems, some of which require lateral thinking.

Open-ended Problems

Suppose that you are to design a timetable for yourself allowing you enough time to complete all the reading assignments for your college courses. This kind of open-ended problem may have more than one workable solution, and lateral thinking can help you generate alternatives, as well as different ways of approaching the problem. For example, it might seem logical for you to begin by determining how many pages you need to read a day. Then you would divide that total by the number of pages you read on average in an hour and so arrive at the number of hours you need to schedule into your daily timetable for reading. When you put your plan into operation and actually spend the scheduled number of hours reading, you may find that you have solved the problem—or, you may find that you have not. By directing your attention to reading, you may have overlooked some crucial factors such as the amount of time you need for attending classes or traveling to classes or socializing or doing your laundry.

By using lateral thinking, however, you might flip the problem of scheduling enough time for reading and look at the matter from other directions. Suppose that you spend all your time reading. What would you have to give up? Now you can start subtracting the number of hours you need to do other things besides reading, and the amount of time you have left may be the solution. This approach may also cause you to question what your needs and priorities really are. The problem may not be that there is not enough time for reading, but that there is too much time spent on other activities.

Lateral thinking is useful because it multiplies possibilities, and encourages us to think of alternatives. In lateral thinking, you can pursue an idea even if it seems silly, because it may lead you to an insight or to a way of restructuring a pattern. For instance, you may think to yourself, "I would have enough time for reading, if only there were another day in the week." At first, this idea seems trivial, and you would likely dismiss it. But suppose that you choose instead to explore it and suspend judgment for the time being. A working day is usually eight hours. Can you free up eight hours in a week by taking a little time here and there from other activities?

Lateral thinking may also prevent us from being trapped in blind alleys. Because we see the timetable problem in terms of the number of hours spent or not spent reading, we may assume that the reading will get done as soon as we allow enough time. The solution must involve determining the correct number of hours to set aside. But what if none of the timetables you might devise actually works? It may be that the timetable itself is a blind alley, and continuing to think in this track becomes increasingly frustrating. Lateral thinking can take us outside the timetable to consider other factors. Maybe you do not enjoy reading and so are looking for ways of avoiding it, or maybe you need to learn some critical reading strategies that will help you make your reading more efficient. Instead of persisting in the effort to plan a workable timetable, you might need to direct your attention to these other factors first. Whenever a problem begins to seem insolvable, lateral thinking becomes a tool for escaping blind alleys and for approaching the problem in a fresh way.

No matter what sort of problem you encounter, your chances of solving it improve if you approach it actively, conscious of the steps you can follow and of the escape routes available to you if the steps become too rigid. John Chaffee outlines a systematic approach to problem solving that consists of five steps:

1. What is the problem?
2. What are the alternatives?
3. What are the advantages and disadvantages of each alternative?
4. What is the solution?
5. How well is the solution working? [2]

2. John Chaffee, *Thinking Critically* (Boston: Houghton Mifflin, 1988) 3.

These five questions, because they are sequential and because they require you to make decisions and judgments as you work through them, are especially suited to vertical thinking. However, you can readily apply lateral thinking when formulating ideas about what the problem is and when generating alternatives. If the solution you eventually choose is flawed when you try to put it into practice, you can return to an earlier alternative. Lateral thinking also allows you to jump ahead in the sequence or to abandon the sequence altogether if it becomes too restrictive. As in the timetable problem, you can flip an apparent solution and look at the situation from the opposite point of view: that is, you can assume that all your time will be spent on reading and then schedule other activities. Or you can begin with an insight solution (creating an extra day in the week) and then work backward from the solution to put it into effect.

You also need to consider the nature of the problems you are likely to encounter in an academic setting or within a specific field of study. Chances are that you will not be asked to solve a logic puzzle in a college composition class. Nor is your history instructor likely to require that you hand in a timetable showing the amount of time you spend reading. Nevertheless, the thinking skills you will need to develop and apply are essentially the same. You will need to think logically and avoid contradictions, to generate ideas and develop them, and to weigh evidence and evaluate other viewpoints or alternatives.

The specific critical thinking strategies outlined in the remainder of this section will help you focus on some of the problems frequently encountered when you are trying to understand and evaluate information. As you work through them, remember that critical thinking is neither an accident nor a gift, but a skill you can develop by being active, open-minded, and conscious of your own thought patterns.

IDENTIFYING BIAS AND TESTING ASSUMPTIONS

Carefully examining your own thinking is a crucial part of becoming a critical thinker. Although no one intends to make errors in thinking, we often overlook our biases, and so fail to recognize one of the most common ways in which thinking can be distorted. The notion of being biased generally has negative connotations, but all of us are biased in the sense that we all have particular beliefs, personal tastes, and preferences. As long as we are aware of our biases, we can make allowances for them in our thinking. Bias becomes a problem when we ignore our convictions and predilections and allow them to lead us into making unreasoned judgments.

Frequently, a personal bias encourages us to accept certain assumptions as fact. For example, if you have ever been caught in a rainstorm and later developed a cold, you might be biased toward accepting as fact a causal relationship between wet clothing and colds. An assumption is merely a belief that something is true—a seeming fact or a statement taken for granted. Just as we all have biases, we all make assumptions in our lives in order to function. However, sometimes these assumptions cut off other avenues of inquiry. Thinking that we already know the cause of colds, we keep warm and dry and spend time visiting friends who have colds. When we later begin to cough and sneeze, we learn too late that a virus can cause colds. To think critically, then, it is necessary to identify bias and to test assumptions, both in our own thinking, and in the thinking of others.

Illustration

Detecting bias and commonly held assumptions can sometimes be a tricky process. To practice your skills in detecting such flaws in thinking, read the following short fable by James Thurber. In this fable, the biases and assumptions are deliberately exaggerated to emphasize how easily people can be tricked by them.

THE RABBITS WHO CAUSED ALL THE TROUBLE

James Thurber

Within the memory of the youngest child there was a family of rabbits who lived near a pack of wolves. The wolves announced that they did not like the way the rabbits were living. (The wolves were crazy about the way they themselves were living, because it was the only way to live.) One night several wolves were killed in an earthquake and this was blamed on the rabbits, for it is well known that rabbits pound on the ground with their hind legs and cause earthquakes. On another night one of the wolves was killed by a bolt of lightning and this was also blamed on the rabbits, for it is well known that lettuce-eaters cause lightning. The wolves threatened to civilize the rabbits if they didn't behave, and the rabbits decided to run away to a desert island. But the other animals, who lived at a great distance, shamed them, saying, "You must stay where you are and be brave. This is no world for escapists. If the wolves attack you, we will come to your aid, in all probability." So the rabbits continued to live near the wolves and one day there was a terrible flood which drowned a great many wolves. This was blamed on the rabbits, for it is well known that carrot-nibblers with long ears cause floods. The wolves descended on the rabbits, for their own good, and imprisoned them in a dark cave, for their own protection.

When nothing was heard about the rabbits for some weeks, the other animals demanded to know what had happened to them. The wolves replied that the rabbits had been eaten and since they had been eaten the affair was a purely internal matter. But the other animals warned that they might possibly unite against the wolves unless some reason was given for the destruction of the rabbits. So the wolves gave them one. "They were trying to escape," said the wolves, "and, as you know, this is no world for escapists."

Moral: Run, don't walk, to the nearest desert island.

Thurber's fable is a delightful lesson in the dangers of biases and assumptions, some of which are more obvious than others. Clearly, the wolves hold some extreme biases, or prejudices, against the rabbits. They label them "lettuce-eaters" and "carrot-nibblers" just as people often stereotype and label groups of other people. This prejudice allows the wolves to make assertions about the rabbits that have no basis in fact and for which there is no evidence: that rabbits cause earthquakes, lightning bolts, and floods.

The other animals, however, have a bias toward bravery (at least in potential victims, if not in themselves) and so assume that staying to fight is, in all cases, better than running away. Fatally for them, the rabbits agree and so abandon their only hope for survival. They assume that the other animals really will come to their aid—"in all probability"—and choose to test this assumption with their very lives. When called to account for their actions, the wolves cleverly manipulate the bias against escapism to their own advantage. Of course, escaping to safety is not quite the same thing as escapism, but since the other animals made no distinction between the two concepts in their advice to the rabbits, they can hardly object now.

Thurber directs the moral of his fable at the reader and makes a general statement of a truth on the basis of the particular events described. This statement may well be the opposite of the reader's own bias in favor of fighting for one's rights. Thus, the entire story invites the reader to examine more carefully his or her own biases and the assumptions that would seem to follow from them. It suggests that in some circumstances escape might be the wiser course. Bias in thinking and the unquestioning acceptance of assumptions can cause us to overlook crucial variables and leap too readily to certain conclusions, just as the rabbits believe too easily that the other animals, with their fine sentiments about bravery, will not abandon them to an unthinkable fate.

The ironic title of the fable, "The Rabbits Who Caused All the Trouble," stresses the extent to which bias can distort clear thinking. By blaming the victims, the title obscures the deliberate aggression of the wolves and the ineffectual behavior of the other animals. Blaming the victim is an error that occurs frequently in thinking because it seems to provide a simple explanation for a complex set of circumstances and because the victim is rarely in a position to challenge the assumption. To be effective critical thinkers, we must examine carefully even those beliefs and assumptions that seem self-evident to us.

Bias in Language

Thurber deliberately reveals biases in order to make the larger point that people sometimes act on assumptions rather than on the basis of evidence and reasoned decisions. But bias in most of the information we receive is rarely so obvious. Because bias is usually hidden, or implicit, detecting bias is sometimes a matter of directing our attention toward how and why information is being delivered to us. One strategy you can use to uncover bias is to pay close attention to word choice, or diction. After all, most professional writers are very skilled in using language both to persuade readers to accept a certain point of view and to hide or discount other points of view.

The attention being paid to sexism in language underscores how word choice and usage can influence people's thoughts and feelings. If language can be used to help make women invisible, as in the term *mankind,* or to denigrate women, as in the difference between the positive male term *bachelor* and the negative female term *spinster,* then language can also be used in many other ways to encourage automatic or unthinking responses. The three kinds of language especially linked to the notion of bias are emotive language, euphemistic language, and advertising language.

Emotive Language

Emotive language stimulates certain feelings in people. In his book *Practical Thinking*, Edward de Bono has a list of what he calls "goody-goody" words, which invite positive reactions and which have become convenient ways of saying that an idea is good, right, proper, and ought to be acted upon.[3] The list includes such words as *honesty, dignity, justice, flexible,* and *responsible.* To this list, Thurber could easily add *bravery:* his fable is an illustration of how the rabbits respond to the goody-goody word without thinking critically. In fact, Thurber says that the rabbits are "shamed" into staying and so drives home the point that we could also make a list of emotive words that could be termed "the baddies." The use of such words would, of course, bias us against accepting a particular idea or action, lest it be too "cowardly," "hasty," "narrow," or (ironically) "biased."

You can make your own list of words likely to evoke strong feelings in yourself and others. Remember, however, that emotive language, in itself, is not problematic; in fact, much of what we read would be much duller without it. Problems occur when emotive language is used to disguise a personal opinion or prejudice as a fact, as when the wolves claim that it is "well known" that rabbits cause earthquakes.

Euphemistic Language

Euphemisms often mask an ugly or painful reality with an innocuous or pleasant appearance. For instance, such phrases as "passed away" and "the dearly departed" help soften the harshness of death. Sometimes, euphemisms are employed to inflate a sense of importance or to imply a certain status, as when a secretary becomes an "administrative assistant" or a head cook becomes a "chef." Euphemisms, however, can also be used to deliberately mislead people and distort reality. For example, in Thurber's fable, the wolves wish to "civilize" the rabbits, a euphemism for conquering and, in all likelihood, killing them.

---

3. Edward de Bono, *Practical Thinking* (London: Penguin Books, 1991) 101.

Besides misdirecting our attention, euphemisms may disguise or justify wrongful acts: the wolves "descended on the rabbits," rather than attacking them, and did so "for their own [the rabbits'] protection." In Western culture, such topics as war, nuclear technology, poverty, racism, politics, and urban and family problems are especially rife with euphemisms. Here are some of the most commonly used:

inner city	apartheid	substance abuse
pink slip	nuclear exchange	political will
underdeveloped	dysfunctional family	corollary damage
curfews	pacification	gentrification

Euphemisms are often effective simply because many people would prefer not to look too closely at some of the more unpleasant realities of life. Yet if we choose to wear the ready-made blinders provided by comforting euphemisms, we are more likely to be fooled into accepting the unacceptable or induced to delay action. Euphemisms warn us to think critically and not to take statements at face value.

Advertising Language

It may seem to you that advertising language is already so exaggerated that no one needs to be warned about it. This bias is precisely what many advertisers wish you to accept. If you believe that the associations made between a product and a certain set of words and images—invariably goody-goody words and images—are silly or outrageous, you are more inclined to turn off your critical thinking frame of mind.

Most experts agree that advertising is effective because it works, at least partially, on an unconscious level. You may well think the associations between products and words are fairly meaningless, but you will still recall those associations, and perhaps remember the name of a certain product, or choose a certain product over another, because of them. For example, you might buy a particular brand of beer because you associate it with great parties and having lots of friends; or you might select a certain brand of hair-coloring product, thinking "I'm worth it." The language of advertising is effective because it appeals to our desires, biases, fears, and insecurities.

Bias and Stereotypes

Besides honing our skills to detect bias in language, we also should learn to recognize stereotypes, which might be described as general statements that encode extreme biases. Most stereotypes cannot stand up to any serious examination, but they are powerful nonetheless because they encourage simplification and categorization. They do so by means of convenient labels or superficial sets of characteristics. Some stereotypes are so ingrained that they prevent us from processing new information or from having insights. For example, if you accept that wolves are bloodthirsty and then watch a nature documentary that provides compelling evidence to the contrary, you are much more likely to discount the evidence than you are to change your mind. When faced with contrary information it is easier to make an exception, than to rethink stereotypes. For instance, it is easier to conclude that wolves are bloodthirsty, *except* perhaps timber wolves, as they have become more accustomed to humans.

Since being open-minded—that is, willing to revise our own biases and predilections—is essential to critical thinking, we need to be honest about the stereotypes we hold. Also, since we often think of stereotypes as negative, we may not detect any positive stereotypical generalizations we tend to make in our thinking—for example, that women are sympathetic or men are strong. Being aware of your own thinking is the first step in improving your thinking.

Testing Assumptions

A bias can cause us to accept certain assumptions as reliable without checking for supporting evidence or reasons. Therefore, the skills of detecting bias and testing assumptions are linked. People tend to find the views of those who agree with them especially compelling and the views of those who disagree with them suspect. In addition, many college students tend to believe that information given to them by experts or by professional writers must be factual and so cannot be challenged. Critical thinkers, however, make no such assumptions and are willing to use specific strategies to test their own thinking, as well as the thinking of others.

Three strategies will help you test assumptions: the evidence check, the "why" and "what's that" strategy, and the "plus,""minus," "interesting," or "speculative" points strategy, known as PMI. As you read about these strategies, apply them to John Rowe Townsend's article "Are Children's Books Racist and Sexist?" Townsend, a British journalist and writer, is an expert on children's literature. While reading his essay, try to identify any patterns of bias in his word choice and any assumptions you think he makes.

ARE CHILDREN'S BOOKS RACIST
AND SEXIST?

John Rowe Townsend

H ugh Lofting, who wrote the Doctor Dolittle books, was allegedly "a white racist and chauvinist, guilty of almost every prejudice known to modern white Western man." William H. Armstrong's *Sounder*, which won the principal American children's book award in 1970 and has been made into a successful film, is denounced as "emasculating" the black man and "destructuring" the black family. Beatrix Potter's *Tale of Peter Rabbit* is described as "perhaps one of the most sexist animal fantasies in children's literature": it "keeps selling and influencing young boys and girls to believe that only males have great adventures and are excitingly 'naughty.'" In *Watership Down*, Richard Adams is said to have "grafted exalted human spirits to the rabbit bodies of his male characters and has made the females mere rabbits. The males are superhuman and the females sub-human."

The first two of these charges are made in articles reprinted in *Racist and Sexist Images in Children's Books*, published by the Writers and Readers Publishing Co-operative and obtainable from Children's Rights Workshop, 73 Balfour Street, London S.E. 17. The third comes from *Sexism in Award Winning Picture Books*, by Suzanne M. Czaplinski, which is also available from CRW. The fourth is from an article by Jane Resh Thomas in America's leading magazine on children's literature, the *Horn Book*, for August 1974.

I will come back to these accusations later. They are just a few among scores of similar charges leveled at well known children's books. The supposedly innocent pastures of children's literature are beginning to look like minefields as one instance after another of alleged racism or sexism is detected and exploded. Why is this happening? How far are such allegations justified? What, if anything, ought authors and publishers to be doing about them?

The campaigns against racism and sexism appear to have got most of their early impetus from the United States. Two articles—not, I think, the first in their fields, but the first to be widely known and quoted, and to make powerful impact—were one by Nancy Larrick in *Saturday Review* for 11 September 1965, on "The All-White World of Children's Books" and one by a collective of "Feminists on Children's Media" in *School Library Journal* for January 1971, called "A Feminist Look at Children's Books."

Nancy Larrick drew attention to the almost complete omission at that time of Negroes, from books for children. Although in some American cities more than half the schoolchildren were black, she found that over a three-year period only four-fifths of one percent of trade books for children from 63 leading publishers told a story about American Negroes today: and that many children's books which did include a Negro showed him as a servant or slave, a sharecropper, a migrant worker or a menial.

Nancy Larrick's article noted incidentally the formation in New York of the Council on Interracial Books for Children. This council has been the source of many studies, ten of which make up the booklet already mentioned on *Racist and Sexist Images*. (Actually, the title is somewhat misleading, as there is only one study of sexism, and that relates to books about Puerto Ricans, few of which books are likely to be found in Britain.)

In 1971 the Feminists on Children's Literature presented what they themselves called a "merciless analysis" of some of the more highly praised children's books, and concluded that there were proportionately far too few books with girls as central characters. They also found that most of the books they examined were either plain sexist—girls and women being exclusively assigned traditional female roles—or "cop-out" books, in which a heroine appears to be developing promisingly but in the end adjusts to the stereotype. Since then pressure groups in both America and Britain have examined a great many books and have made similar charges.

The assumption, explicit or implicit, of those who are concerned about racism or sexism in children's books is that the books children read affect their attitudes. This assumption is not, so far as I know, based on the results of any organized research. I have not been able to trace any study which has produced substantial evidence of a formative effect. It would in fact be extremely difficult to set up a valid research project. Effects of books on attitudes are hard to isolate and to measure, and at best there would have to be a good deal of reliance on subjective assessment.

It seems fair however to suppose that if stereotypes of racial characteristics or the roles of the sexes are constantly presented to children, they must to some extent be absorbed. (And in any case, ordinary decency suggests that people should not be demeaned for being of the "wrong" sex or color, even if no actual harm can be proved.) At the same time, common sense indicates that children's attitudes will be formed by the whole atmosphere of their society: books are only a rather small part of most children's environment, and children's books indeed tend to reflect the attitudes of society at large rather than to shape them.

Much good has probably been done by pressure groups in causing publishers to think hard about unconscious racism and sexism in school readers, textbooks, and information books. But when we come to creative literature for children I begin to feel serious doubts, especially where there appears to be determined fault-finding. Rather curiously, the greater part of the material I have seen on racism and sexism has concerned itself with children's "quality" fiction and picture books: hardly any has tackled films or television, though some work has been done on comics and series-books. I say "curiously" because one might have thought that television and films were much more popular, insistent, and influential media than books. Also, to be frank about it, "quality" books are largely read in the kind of homes where parents and children are least likely to take their opinions at second hand from outside.

It's hard to avoid suspecting that books may well be scrutinized in preference to films or television because books are handy and stay still while you look at them. One also wonders whether good books may be investigated rather than poor ones because good books are more interesting for the investigator. Who wants to spend months researching the Famous Five or the Bobbsey Twins? In America, the books that win major awards have been particularly thoroughly worked over, sometimes with disconcerting results.

The introduction to the booklet on *Racist and Sexist Images* says, over the signatures of the Children's Rights Workshop in London, that "we can no longer base critical assessment solely on literary merit. Content and values, explicit or implicit, deserve similar critical attention." And in a statement on Children's Books, CRW (to which, incidentally, I am indebted for the sight of a good deal of material) says: "We maintain that, in any critical assessment of a children's book, its message and social values are all-important; at least, they concern us more than the criteria of style, beauty, or form." I think there is a misconception here of the nature of literary criticism. It seems to be implied that the literary merit with which critics are concerned is a kind of ornamentation: the turrets and twiddles of a building rather than its structure. But in fact every self-respecting critic is concerned with the book as a whole: of course its content and values deserve and receive attention: it's merely that a good critic will refuse to take a narrow monocular view.

And when one finds articles, such as one in *Interracial Books for Children*, vol. 5, no. 3 (1974) on showing children how to detect racism and sexism in a book, one must surely feel uneasy. Is this not itself a racist or sexist activity, creating the kind of division it purports to oppose?

To my mind, the literature on this subject includes too many wild generalizations made by people who obviously haven't read enough books or have managed only to see what they are determined to see. When they come down to the actual cases, the humorlessness and stridency of campaigners often make it easy—perhaps too easy—to pour scorn. Pat Hutchinson's *Rosie's Walk*, a marvelously funny picture book featuring a hen who walks around the farmyard totally unaware that a fox is after her, while the fox is comically thwarted at every turn, has been attacked because a hen is seen as a symbol of stupid womanhood. With similar lack of humor it is suggested, seriously, in America that Cinderella should be rewritten in a less sexist vein:

> Cinderella is pleasing in appearance, but as she spends much of her time at household labor, her body bears the signs: dishpan hands and flat feet. At the ball, she is interested in meeting as many new and interesting people as she can, and during the evening she dances with many men. Since she knows that the coach will turn into a pumpkin if she doesn't leave before the stroke of twelve, she plans her exit well in advance. . . .

Sometimes it seems that authors just can't win. Pippi Longstocking, the independent self-assertive supergirl in a series of books by Astrid Lindgren, might appear to be a feminist dream: but no, a writer in *Interracial Books for Children* has seen through her:

> It is soon apparent that Pippi isn't a girl at all, even a tomboy, but a boy in disguise. Astrid Lindgren has simply equipped Pippi with all the traits we have come to think of as male . . . Pippi acts like a "real" man.

One of the dangers of the sillier and wilder attacks is that they are counter-productive, provoking ridicule and diverting attention from the genuinely difficult cases, of which there are several. A well known one is that of *Little Black Sambo*, first published in 1899. His author, Helen Bannerman, certainly meant no harm: her trouble was that she couldn't draw very well and was a bit confused about the races anyway. Sambo's crudely drawn features have given offense to large numbers of nonwhites, but he has also given great pleasure to many children, including nonwhites. Should he be removed from library shelves in this country, as in the United States? There are arguments both ways, and I do not seek to resolve them here.

Of the books mentioned in my opening paragraph, *The Story of Doctor Dolittle*, which dates from 1920, does undoubtedly contain offensive facetious references to blacks. Hugh Lofting obviously saw them as comic figures; his own drawings make that clear. Like Mrs. Bannerman, he meant no harm; he was in fact a sincere internationalist, and his views on race were advanced for his day, but he lacked foresight and sensitivity. He leaves us with a problem.

The main objection to *Sounder*, as I understand it, is that it shows an oppressed black family as spiritless and submissive, rather than actively fighting injustice. But these were poor, ignorant, friendless people, and the setting is a good many years in the past; to me, as to many other commentators, the story has the ring of truth. The attack on Peter Rabbit is too silly to need refutation; but the criticism of *Watership Down* from which I quoted—and which incidentally does not seek to condemn the whole book—is sensible and cogent; it would be a pity if it were met with yawns or instant resentment.

Another danger is that—as is already happening to some extent—authors and editors run scared and go to absurd lengths to avoid giving offense. (An American editor rejected *Polar*, a picture book about a toy polar bear which is published in England by Andre Deutsch, on the ground that the text, written by Elaine Moss, states explicitly that the bear is white.) A demand to avoid stereotypes can easily become in effect a demand for a different stereotype: for instance that girls should always be shown as strong, brave and resourceful, and that mothers should always have jobs and never, never wear an apron. And books written to an approved formula, or with deliberate didactic aim, do not often have the breath of life. Some members of women's groups in North America have published their own anti-sexist books, featuring such characters as fire-fighting girls or boys who learn to crochet. Good luck to them; but those I have seen are far below professional standard.

It seems to me that authors and publishers should avoid on the one hand jumping hastily on to the bandwagon, and on the other hand reacting over-sensitively and negatively to criticism. They should consider suggestions and complaints on their merits, act on them where action is justified and possible, but also be prepared to reject unfounded condemnation. They have, it is true, a responsibility to children and to society in general: they also have an obligation to practice their craft as best they can, to tell the truth as they see it, and to hold on to artistic freedom for themselves and their successors.

The Evidence Check

In argumentative essays, assumptions are unproved or unsupported statements, so the first test is simply to check for evidence, reasons, and illustrations. You will also need to make some judgments in weighing the kinds of evidence you might find. Ask yourself any of these three questions:

- Is the reason or illustration convincing?
- How reliable is the source of information?
- Is the evidence accurate?

Let us first consider an unsupported statement in Townsend's essay. One of Townsend's purposes for writing is to determine whether allegations of sexism and racism in children's books are justified. He discusses, with some skepticism, the extent to which books can influence children's attitudes, and he points out that studies done on racism and sexism tend to focus on "quality" or award-winning fiction. Then he makes the following statement: "Also, to be frank about it, 'quality' books are largely read in the kind of homes where parents and children are least likely to take their opinions at second hand from outside."

This statement is offered in support of the larger point that racist and sexist images in books have not been proven to affect the attitudes of children. How reliable is this statement as evidence? Does Townsend offer any proof that "quality" books are usually found only in the homes of critical thinkers? Even though he is an expert on children's literature, does that expertise extend to making generalizations about what kinds of books are likely to be read in what kinds of homes? Clearly, the answer to these questions is "no." In fact, Townsend is making an assumption, and offers no proof to support it. A mere assumption, no matter how convincingly written, is poor evidence.

Now, let us examine a second statement which appears near the end of the essay. At this point, Townsend is concerned that oversensitivity to racism and sexism can be just as harmful as a lack of sensitivity. He writes: "Another danger is that—as is already happening to some extent—authors and editors run scared and go to absurd lengths to avoid giving offense."

This time, Townsend does offer convincing support for his claim. He gives the example of a book about a toy polar bear, which was not published because the story "states explicitly that the bear is white." In this case, the example suitably fits the charge of absurdity, and is confined to the exact area of Townsend's expertise. There may be other points you could raise and other examples you could think of to challenge

Townsend's point of view, but this statement passes the evidence check and cannot be easily dismissed as an assumption. In learning to apply the evidence check, you will not only become more skilled in distinguishing between assumptions and arguments, but also more comfortable in making sensible judgments about the worthiness and reliability of evidence.

The "Why" and "What's That" Strategy

To work, assumptions depend on the notion that some ideas are so obvious and so taken for granted that they do not need to be explained. Assumptions pretend to be "givens." Thus, the two questions featured in this strategy have been deliberately chosen to challenge the obvious and to expose the passive sort of thinking that takes things for granted.

Edward de Bono explains the "why" technique as a tool of lateral thinking used "to create discomfort with any explanation."[4] The purpose of this strategy is not to arrive at a correct explanation, nor to defend a point, but to explore it. If you have ever been with a child who repeatedly asks "why" in response to a long-accepted but unexamined explanation for something, then you have probably experienced just how startling this simple question can sometimes be.

Similarly, the question, "What's that?" punctures the assumption that a frequently used phrase or concept means the same thing to everyone. Furthermore, it is not unlikely that the concept you will be challenging belongs on a goody-goody list, and so it has the added connotation of being admirable and justified.

Illustration

Note that, in discussing racism and sexism in children's books, Townsend distinguishes between creative literature and school readers, textbooks, and information books. He does not explain why he makes this distinction, perhaps assuming that the reason is obvious. You can explore this matter by applying the "why" technique as follows:

Why is creative literature a different case from readers and textbooks?

Maybe works of fiction are not intended to transmit facts in the same way as information books; instead they entertain, tell a story, or convey a point of view.

---

4. de Bono, *Lateral Thinking* 91.

Why do they do that?

One reason is so we can understand other people or other experiences beyond our own immediate horizons.

Why is that understanding important?

That is one of the ways we learn, because we can't know everything firsthand. Unless we are willing to listen to the voices of others and learn from their experiences, we must settle for knowing only a narrow slice of life.

A further "why" raised here would probably invite a repetition of the point that we cannot know everything firsthand. The "why" questions should stop once the ideas you are generating become repetitive.

Now consider the ideas just generated, which indicate that we learn from others about experiences beyond our own. Is it not possible that we could also learn racist and sexist attitudes? Townsend's special case for creative literature seems shaky, and so this part of his argument needs to be challenged.

You can apply the "what's that?" question to Townsend's concluding sentence and, indeed, to much of his concluding paragraph. He argues that authors and publishers do need to be sensitive to racism and sexism, but that they also need to protect "artistic freedom." What's that? Once you are willing to raise this question, a number of other questions immediately come to mind. Who defines artistic freedom? Are sexist and racist images acceptable within this frame of reference? Are racism and sexism okay as long as such ideas are part of an imaginative and well-written story?

No matter what questions you ask or what answers you think are reasonable, the initial "what's that?" challenge alerts you to the fact that Townsend is not being specific, but is merely relying on a goody-goody bias. A closer examination of the final paragraph indicates other equally vague and impractical ideas. For example, he concludes his argument by urging authors and publishers to be wise and balanced in their decisions. This advice sounds reasonable and perhaps even beyond challenge. But what does this advice mean? How can it be put into practice?

The PMI

The PMI (which, as mentioned earlier, stands for "plus," "minus," and "interesting" or "speculative" points) is a critical thinking tool invented by de Bono to prevent people from making judgments that are too hasty. When we believe that we are correct or that we have found the right solution to a problem, we are likely to assume that there is no need to think further. There is also the danger that we will be biased toward accepting an answer we favor and so make a judgment before giving the opposite point of view fair consideration.

The PMI is quite simple to do, and because it involves a specific sequence of activity, it is likely to be more effective than the vague admonition to think fairly. To do a PMI, you first write down a proposition, or hypothesis, and then examine it by thinking about its advantages (plus points), then its disadvantages (minus points), and, finally, any interesting or speculative points that occur to you that cannot be labeled either pluses or minuses. As de Bono recommends, practice learning how to use the tool on a silly proposition first. For example, he uses the suggestion that people should wear badges to indicate what sort of mood they are in.[5] What would some plus points be? What would the minus points be? What interesting ideas occur to you about this suggestion?

Here is a sample of what a PMI on this proposition might look like:

Plus

1. You could avoid people in bad moods.
2. You could decide by checking a person's badge whether this was a good time to ask for a favor.
3. You would be especially caring if a friend was wearing a sad badge.

Minus

1. You would need a lot of badges if you experience lots of moods.
2. People are good at hiding their moods; in order to trick others, they might not wear the correct badge.
3. You might lose the badge you are wearing. Can a person be moodless?

Interesting or Speculative

1. How is it that we determine another person's mood without needing badges?
2. Would badges be an invasion of privacy for some people?
3. There is a lot of pressure put on people to be happy all the time. Would wearing badges make it easier for people to be honest about their feelings?

When doing a PMI, remember that the goal is to develop the habit of suspending judgment until you have looked at an issue from more

5. Edward de Bono, *Teaching Thinking* (London: Penguin Books, 1991) 162–164.

than one point of view. Now try to do a PMI on an issue stemming from Townsend's article.

One of the unresolved questions that Townsend raises in his essay is whether racist and sexist children's books should be removed from library shelves. Although you probably have an idea already of how you might handle this dilemma, suspend your judgment long enough to do a PMI. The following example can guide you.

Proposition: Racist and sexist children's books should be removed from library shelves.

Plus

1. A clear message would be sent to authors, editors, and publishers about eliminating offensive material.
2. Children would have more positive role models.
3. As public institutions, libraries would be fulfilling a responsibility to be politically correct.

Minus

1. Less knowledge of racism and sexism means developing fewer strategies to cope with it.
2. Forbidden books have a tendency to seem more appealing. People may read them because their curiosity will have been aroused.
3. Where would the censorship stop?

Interesting or Speculative

1. The focus here is on reading racist and sexist books. Even if we could control that, how do we monitor the attitudes of people who write this stuff or who believe it anyway?
2. Should we make any distinctions between books from long ago and current books? I think it's important to understand the context of the past, including its racism and sexism, in order to understand the present.
3. Would we be treating the symptom or the disease? I'm not sure availability versus censorship is the problem.

The person who did this particular PMI decided, on the basis of the points generated, that the books should not be removed from the library shelf. A different set of points might have led to a different conclusion. Whatever answer emerges when you do a PMI, you will at least know that you have tried to reduce the effects of bias and to think through an issue fairly, without assuming that the answer is either inevitable or obvious.

BIZARRO By DAN PIRARO

Exploring Issues from Multiple Perspectives

The cartoon above demonstrates that people can witness the same event or consider the same problem and yet have very different views. In fact, we perceive ourselves and the world around us in ways that reflect our own experiences, knowledge, and individual personalities. We are also selective about what we perceive, as indicated by the person who holds up a sign saying he was not paying attention and so, in a sense, saw nothing.

The concept of varying perspectives—how we select, organize, and interpret the stimuli around us—is often explained by means of the metaphor of wearing different spectacles, or viewing the world through different lenses. To become an effective critical thinker, it is important to be aware of both your own lenses and those of others. Exploring an issue from multiple perspectives means that you can multiply your opportunities to see more and to learn more from the views of others. Besides enriching your own perspective, this kind of active exploration can also minimize distortions in thinking caused by bias. Imagine that you could sometimes trade your own spectacles for a kaleidoscope—you could see different patterns, different colors, multiple shapes and forms. Looking at an issue from multiple perspectives is rather like seeing something through a kaleidoscope: you can explore different angles, different patterns of thought, and different shades of meaning.

In an academic context, different fields of study have their own special lenses. A psychologist would probably select, organize, and interpret the rhetoric of an election campaign very differently from a political scientist. A marine biologist would likely perceive waves lapping along the shoreline of a lake in a way that a poet would not. Part of your responsibility as a student is to be sensitive to the kinds of issues and information that your academic discipline selects as important and to note the ways in which a particular field of study organizes and interprets data. This task will be easier for you if you are aware that such specialized lenses exist and if you have gained some practice in shifting your own perspectives.

College students often face recurring thinking tasks linked to the concept of multiple perspectives. Three of the most common tasks are as follows:

1. How to cope with the apparently conflicting views of experts
2. How to generate multiple perspectives
3. How to shift your own patterns of thinking

For each of these thinking tasks, you can apply a specific strategy to help you become an effective critical thinker.

Dealing with the Differing Perspectives of Experts

Students often experience confusion when faced with the conflicting views of two or more experts. If expert A is right, how can expert B also be right, and should you agree with one or the other, both, or neither? This confusion is often heightened by the fact that both expert A and expert B seem very convincing, and both have a certain authority by virtue of their expertise.

One way to begin dealing with the confusion is to recognize that the situation is not a matter of being right or wrong, but a matter of differing perspectives. Expert A selects, organizes, and interprets information from a particular perspective; expert B can examine the same issue from another perspective and so reach different conclusions. Your task is not to determine who is right or wrong, but to examine each perspective carefully, to consider both its strengths and limitations, and to explore ways in which the two perspectives might interrelate.

Suppose that in researching the topic of racism and sexism in children's literature for your social science class you read two articles: one by John Rowe Townsend and one by Elaine Batcher and Alison Winter. The perspectives of these experts seem irreconcilable, as is evident by the titles they have chosen. Townsend's title—"Are Children's Books Racist and Sexist?"—seems to leave the entire issue open to debate, whereas Batcher and Winter's title—"Nothing Special: The Portrayal of Girls and Women in Current Junior Grade Readers"—appears to leave little room for doubt, at least as far as sexism is concerned. How can you reconcile these two perspectives, and is it possible to learn from both?

Illustration

"NOTHING SPECIAL": THE PORTRAYAL OF GIRLS AND WOMEN IN CURRENT JUNIOR GRADE READERS

Elaine Batcher and Alison Winter

One insight I have gained from my research among adolescents is that the most ignominious insult with which one can offend a person is to speak of her or him as "nothing special."[1] A short walk through any shopping mall where young people gather will confirm the truth of this, as clothing, comportment and possessions all attest to teenagers' efforts to be both acceptable in the style of a particular group, and in some way special within this selected style. Those who have no group or individual style to highlight them are considered to be "nothing special." Damned or merely excluded, they are ignored.

In a recently conducted study commissioned by the Federation of Women Teachers' Associations of Ontario (FWTAO),[2] a major finding repeats and confirms eleven-year-old data indicating that "nothing special" is about as much as girls and women can ever attain as characters in Junior grade Readers. The study was a deliberate return to subject matter addressed initially in 1975.[3] Once again, Readers approved for use in Junior grade classrooms by the Ontario Ministry of Education in *Circular 14* were evaluated for their portrayal of women and men, girls and boys, as possible role models or conveyors of messages about life's possibilities to children in grades 4, 5, and 6. Sample books from each Reader series were read in entirety, categorized and evaluated along several dimensions.

The first set of criteria dealt with the frequency with which each character type (woman, man, girl, boy) was represented in primary, secondary and background positions, or in a shared story, within Fiction, Character Non-Fiction (all non-fiction referring to people or mentioning gender), and Myth, and the number of times poems and illustrations were female- or male-oriented. The highest counts on the average and for almost every criterion, in almost every Reader series, were found to be those for boys and men. Fictional stories were most frequently about boys, myths and non-fictional material were overwhelmingly about men. While girls were allowed a modicum of representation, women were scarcely there at all. Similarly, poems and pictures were far more likely to be about males than females. With the exclusion of Myths, poems and pictures, which were not counted in the earlier study, these were essentially the findings of 1975.

The second set of criteria inquired into the presentation of each of the character types. Three scales, developed and adapted from literature and the social sciences, were applied where possible to a major female and male character in each story. The self-actualization scale (adapted from Atwood)[4] and the legalistic moral development scale (from Kohlberg)[5] were used in the previous study. Because of recent doubts cast on the universality of Kohlberg's work, we used also a scale distilled from the work of Gilligan and termed it the affiliative moral development scale.[6] While the variation on all three scales was more limited than it was on the first two scales in 1975, indicating more similarity of character presentation than previously, the average presentations, overall and within most series, of women, men, girls and boys, were different.

Women, although usually depicted as more "moral" than men, especially on the affiliative scale, were shown as less self-actualized. The average girls' scores on all three scales were higher than those of boys. Reader/girls were often shown as achieving their goals (self-actualization), and often shown as doing the right thing for the right reason (moral development). This was not the case in 1975 and would appear encouraging. When we looked further at the contents of the stories, however, there was evidence which did not appear in these numbers.

In a single Reader, selected at random from among the Readers with the greatest diversity of content material,[7] girls were seen to perform 26 tasks as compared to boys' 11 tasks. While the boys' tasks included handling equipment, playing piano, dancing, arguing, collecting stickers and protecting mussels, girls were seen to become afflicted with the vanity of city girls, fracture the English language, abandon ballet recital, go on a diet, dream sad dreams and cry soundlessly. In the same book there were 45 activities for men and 15 for women. Men's activities were such things as investigating a kidnapping, writing memoirs, acting in silent films and operating a restaurant chain. Women's activities were such things as being a loyal and true friend, eyeing a letter suspiciously, bossing the neighborhood and being laid up with a sick headache. Boys and men would have opportunities to excel here. But no matter how well and with what intent the girls and women accomplished their activities, these characters could never be special, unless we count as special that slight moral "elevation" with which Victorian men damned women to keep them out of the world of action.

Story plots were another indication of the differences in treatments of females and males, specifically in the relative nature of the challenges set for each. While boys were asked, albeit unrealistically, to take upon their shoulders the adult burdens of saving a drowning man and killing a bear, a girl was given very little to achieve. At best, she might be mistaken for a boy and earn a place on the hockey team, at worst she had to endure captivity and hope her father would soon save her from the sasquatches. Even though the treatment of boys was artificial, boys' maxi-achievements stood in contrast to the also artificial but mini-achievements of girls. In stories about boys, something happened and boys were seen to make it happen. In stories about girls, if something happened, it wasn't much of an event. This should be understood in conjunction with the fact that there were relatively few stories about girls.

There were some stories when a girl or woman was seemingly featured, and these should be discussed for the ways in which they included a female but gave her minimal representation. The only child in a story centering on three men was named "Leslie," and the only indication of her sex was the one picture in which she appeared with long hair.[8] The child captured by the sasquatch was simply a screen on which to project the events of the plot about these mythical creatures.[9] The title character, "The Lady with the Missing Finger," was a device to begin the unfolding of the real tale, a detective story with historical and sea themes which began with her death.[10] These females were in the stories, but their presence was not the highlight of events.

In those relatively few cases where a female was both featured as a central character and essential to the plot, it was frequently the case that the plot worked actively against her being seen as special in any way. At times, this was a simple defeat, such as in the story of the pioneer woman who made pemmican from an entire buffalo, and instead of being congratulated for her effort and success, was given two more buffalo to process.[11] At times, the story took a tortuous route to deliver the message. A young girl given the responsibility of looking after her grandfather's antique shop was shown as overcoming a series of challenges in creative ways. But in the end, her grandfather dressed up in a suit of armor deliberately to scare her and show the reader that here was a normal girl after all—frightened and defeated.[12] Both of these stories, incidentally, were presented as humor.

After thousands of pages of reading, we felt immersed in a medium we came to know and understand as The Old Metaphor (TOM). This was the viewpoint through which every story was told. It was as if all of human existence had to be seen, digested, processed and finally given back to us, the readers, by a man, an old but timeless man, a man who tells us his story. We know this story. We have been listening to it for thousands of years.

TOM is a male-dominated view of the world in which dualism— "either/or" thinking—holds sway. Men name things and thereby call them into creation. Men decide the future of the world and "men's" (meaning people's) place in it. Important values are those of men. Emotion is limited to that which is "appropriate" for either sex. Men may shed a tear for the bloodless sinking of a ship, for example, but would be expected to remain dry-eyed at a family funeral. Boys are men-in-training who must be toughened and readied to inherit the world, whether they want it or not. Women, where they exist, are always "other." Girls can function as ersatz boys or airheads, but what they might become if allowed a full existence is unknown and unexplored.

This was the force of our reading. Stories primarily about boys, and non-fiction pieces featuring men's achievements, and myths about men who were gods or were given godly powers, all lent credence to The Old Metaphor. In 1975, TOM was deeply ingrained on every page. The influence of TOM in the 1986 books was somewhat more subtle, but still there. It was there in the imbalance of numbers; it was there in the imbalanced presentation of activities and story plots and achievements and emotions. Our report called for recognition of TOM as dated and limiting, and for some massive changes in the Readers to embody new metaphors, many new viewpoints of existence. We rejected minimal changes, such as pictures of girls with jeans and mothers who hold jobs outside the home, as simply reinforcing TOM with current appearances.

There is a clue to these new metaphors in this concept of being spe-

cial. I have written elsewhere that it is the task of adolescence to find
something that one likes to do and that one does well.[13] The finding of
such a talent or skill might be seen to make one special. It would seem
to me that the message that one can and should be special is aimed at
the boys who will read the stories, but not at the girls. It would seem to
me, and I have tried here to show, that the message aimed at girls is that
they are *not* special, and they are never to get it into their heads that they
might be. I want to illustrate this point with a series of examples.

There is, in one of the newest Readers, a story about a little girl who
loves to dance, so much so that she dances all day, everywhere she
goes.[14] The story does not point her toward the possibility of a shining
future as a dancer, nor toward the more easily attainable but still attractive hope of keeping dance as an interest that enriches her life. Perhaps
the editors felt they were tired of stories about ballerinas, as indeed
they might be, since dance seems one of the few acceptable "careers"
for girls and has been overdone in Readers. Instead, we are told the girl
is constantly wearing out her shoes and is a nuisance to her family.

When her mother takes her shopping for new shoes, a mysterious
man gives her an unusual-looking pair and says they will make her
walk on clouds. She protests that she does not want to walk on clouds
and is told, "Nonsense! That's what they all say at first, and then they
end up loving it." Her magic slippers make her dance all night and forget where she has been in the morning. Now compliant and conform-
ing, she dances only at her dance class and is no longer a nuisance to
others.

We considered this story to be one of the poorest of offerings to
young minds that we came across. Denise, the "heroine" of the story, is
not special at all. She serves as a vehicle to show that compliance and
conformity are valued in girls, and headstrong interests of the sort
needed to make a success at anything are not. A strange man, given
credibility and power by the story and by the mother within it, is
allowed to impose his way with the girl by way of an exotic gift which
she refuses but is made to accept. If not physical violation (which the
shoes may represent), then spiritual violation occurs. The mother offers
no defense of her daughter and, by her acquiescence is shown as
accepting of the male culture which would force such attentions on her
child. Proof of our construct of the meaning of this story is the detail
that she is made to forget what transpired while she was sleeping.

Contrast the treatment of Denise with that of the twelve-year-old
boy hero of the recent film, "Flight of the Navigator." His creators have
given him exciting adventures in a magical place, the future. He
remembers his experiences and they have enriched his life, *and* he is

allowed to bring back a treasure from that other place to keep for himself—a small, living space-creature whose life he saves and who will be his friend on earth. Poor Denise would have been richer for even one of these blessings, but she gets nothing save the dubious pleasure of cloud-walking. She was not allowed to bring home treasures, even though she intended them as gifts to others. And she is certainly nothing special. The story flattens her. She is no longer a nuisance to others and "she walks down the street just like you and I."

The intention of making a female "normal" was the rationale behind all those kitchen photos of post-war movie stars. Their lives were so far beyond the realm of "normal" women's existence that studios believed the only way they could be made acceptable to the general population was to show them cooking for their men, and thus "normal" women, just like all the women in North America.

This flattening of women is an image Carol Hill's novel *The Eleven Million Mile High Dancer* acknowledges and deliberately shatters.[15] The heroine, Amanda, is described as "America's leading lady astronaut," and as "An astronaut, a physicist, and an extremely good pilot." Her specialness is presented in the following way:

> Sometimes [Amanda] thought of it in this way: I've been
> picked. Just like Copernicus got picked. Everybody who
> has something important and different to do gets picked.
> And it's me. ME!

Hill is obviously speaking the language we wish Readers were speaking. She quotes Coleridge, *Anima Poetae*, at the start:

> If a man could pass through Paradise in a dream, and have
> a flower presented to him as a pledge that his soul had
> really been there, and if he found that flower in his hand
> when he woke—the Ay!—and what then?

The gift of flower or spaceling empowers "he" who has received it. He is special. Hill's heroine Amanda is special—she has been picked. Denise will never be special, and it is Denise whose story young girls and boys will read.

There are many affirmations of manhood in the stories children read, but few if any affirmations of womanhood. Girls who read the stories in school Readers are forced to make daily identifications with boys and men in self-betraying ways. This cannot make them feel very good about themselves. We do not think this is the way things should be. Perhaps the gaffes in the stories mirror gaps in our knowledge of what girlhood and womanhood are in life. But isn't literature supposed to allow us to work through these things? Shouldn't our children be led to explore the possibilities of their existence through the experiences of others? Shouldn't school books affirm life rather than deny it? We think so. And we wish that people in the textbook industry would catch onto this a little faster. We are insulting and betraying so many children through their errors.

1. See for example, Elaine Batcher, "Building the Barriers: Adolescent Girls Delimit the Future," in Greta Hofmann Nemiroff (Ed.), *Women and Men: Interdisciplinary Readings on Gender* (Toronto: Fitzhenry and Whiteside, 1987), pp. 150–164.

2. For a full report of the findings see E. Batcher, A. Winter and V. Wright, *The More Things Change . . .* Available for purchase from FWTAO, 1260 Bay Street, Toronto M5R 2B8.

3. E. Batcher, D. Brackstone, A. Winter, V. Wright, *. . . And Then There Were None* (Toronto: FWTAO, 1975).

4. Margaret Atwood, *Survival* (Toronto: Anansi, 1972).

5. As decribed by Nancy Porter and Nancy Taylor in *How to Assess the Moral Reasoning of Students* (Toronto, OISE, 1972).

6. Carol Gilligan, *In a Different Voice* (Cambridge, Mass.: Harvard University Press, 1982).

7. *Star Flights* (Toronto: Nelson, 1984).

8. "Passing Thro'," in *Star Flights* (above).

9. "Karen's Diary," in *Zap: Monsters* (Toronto: Fitzhenry and Whiteside, 1981).

10. "The Lady With the Missing Finger," in *Yesterstories: The Lady With the Missing Finger* (Toronto: Globe/Modern, 1979).

11. "Pemmican by the Pound," in *Pingo* (Toronto: Gage, 1980).

12. "Ghosts Are Braver Than People," in *Driftwood and Dandelions* (Toronto: Nelson, 1970).

13. Elaine Batcher, "Building the Barriers," above.

14. "Denise, the Little Dancer With Big Feet," in *Flip Flops* (Toronto: Nelson, 1983).

15. Carol Hill, *The Eleven Million Mile High Dancer* (New York: Penguin, 1986).

Your first task is to identify the perspective in each case and then consider both the strengths and limitations of each perspective. Normally, you would have access to context notes or brief author biographies, which would enable you to determine a specific perspective: Townsend is an author of children's books, whereas Batcher is a researcher and writer in education, and Winter is a teacher. That information alone makes it evident that the experts are wearing different spectacles. It can hardly be surprising if an author of children's books considers the issue of racism and sexism from a different angle than two educators. You might also consider it reasonable that the two female authors would be especially concerned with sexist images, but be careful not to assume that their conclusions are therefore biased.

The next task is to determine how the authors' perspectives have shaped the ways in which they select, organize, and interpret data. Townsend concentrates on creative literature, or fiction; Batcher and Winter focus on junior grade Readers. This selection process makes some sense, given the authors' respective areas of expertise. Other differences in selection include Townsend's stronger emphasis on racism than on sexism and on well-known or award-winning fiction. Townsend also raises the question of whether children's attitudes are affected by books and points to the likelihood of a greater influence being felt from television and film. Again, this selection of data makes sense, given the doubts raised by the question format of his title.

In addition, the authors base their findings on different studies of children's literature. Townsend cites material available from the Children's Rights Workshop in England, as well as three American articles. Batcher and Winter have a very specific focus and are updating a study of educational Readers, originally conducted in 1975, by the Federation of Women Teachers' Associations of Ontario, Canada. From this information, you might infer that Townsend is writing for a more general audience than that of Batcher and Winter. The two co-authors seem to be directing their remarks primarily to teachers and to the administrators who have approved the Readers under study.

Once you have identified the focus of each essay, you can begin to consider some of the strengths and limitations of each perspective. Townsend discusses *Sounder* and *Watership Down,* well-known books you may have read already. Thus, you may be able to balance some of his conclusions against your own. His essay, although very tentative in its conclusions, provides useful information about racist images and raises the point that good politics do not always result in good books; many antisexist books are dull precisely because they are written to formula. An author himself, Townsend reveals some of the concerns of writers and publishers that might otherwise be overlooked. The major limitation of Townsend's perspective is that it seems highly personal, and he often does not provide evidence indicating why he finds some allegations exaggerated.

On the other hand, Batcher and Winter do list very specific categories they have used to measure sexism, and, although their focus is restricted, they offer quantitative evidence to support their findings. They actually count the activities for men and women found in the Readers, and offer comparative numbers. They also provide qualitative evidence by means of numerous plot summaries and quotations from the Readers. Batcher and Winter also mention a positive model for girls to read, a novel by Carol Hill, and they carefully explain the ways in which this novel avoids the sexism of the other stories cited. The limitations of Batcher and Winter's perspective include the fact that they are writing for a professional audience and so do not always define their terms. Few general readers will know what "self-actualization," "moral development," and "affiliative moral development" scales mean, and these scales are not explained.

Your final task is to consider ways in which the experts' perspectives interrelate and what you have learned by reading both articles. Batcher and Winter fill in a gap left by Townsend, who chooses not to discuss school Readers or textbooks; and Townsend fills in a gap by providing information about racist images. Townsend refers to pressure groups, and the Batcher and Winter essay is a good example of that voice. By reading both essays, you enrich your own perspective: you can now include different kinds of children's literature and the different concerns of authors, teachers, and educators in your thinking about the issue.

The essential part of this strategy is to remember that you are exploring different perspectives in order to stretch your own: your goal at this point is not to determine which of the experts is right or wrong, but to listen as openly as possible to different points of view. By doing so, you are far more likely to avoid feeling confused about any disagreements and far more likely to begin raising questions of your own left unanswered by the experts. For example, you might be curious enough to read some children's literature published very recently to see for yourself how different minorities and genders are portrayed, or you might want to investigate American junior grade Readers in terms of the categories provided by Batcher and Winter. When you are willing to stretch your own perspectives, you are beginning to take an active step toward thinking in creative and independent ways.

Generating Multiple Perspectives

Sometimes, instead of seeking relationships among differing perspectives provided by experts, you will be asked to examine a problem or an idea from a range of perspectives that you must generate your-self. By generating a range of views on a topic, you protect yourself from thinking too narrowly, and you may discover some pertinent information that might otherwise be overlooked. This technique also improves your ability to evaluate your own ideas or the solutions you might offer to a problem. You can test your ideas against a range of views instead of leaping too quickly to what seems the simplest or easiest conclusion.

Role-playing is a very effective strategy for generating multiple perspectives because it asks you to empathize with or anticipate the concerns of others. In taking on the role of another person, you are essentially trying to look at an issue through that person's lenses, or what you imagine those lenses to be. In most cases, you can use your own experience and knowledge to assume a particular role; however, there may be times when a role is so specialized that you would need to do some research in order to assume it well. Also, role-playing is an example of lateral thinking; therefore, the object is to generate a wealth of perspectives rather than to judge them.

Illustration

Suppose that in response to reading the articles by Townsend and Batcher and Winter you decide that racist and sexist images should be banned from school Readers. You now want to look more closely at the implications of that decision by imaginatively assuming the roles of as many concerned parties as you can and by jotting down some of the comments they might make or questions they might raise. Here is an example of what your list might look like.

A teacher:	A ban curtails academic freedom; I might want to use images from Readers to teach students how to detect and overcome prejudice.
An administrator:	The school will have to buy new Readers. Who is going to pay for this?
An author:	I want to write a story about a group of children who find a magic basketball and win a championship—do the players all have to be girls now? Do I have the knowledge to write about racial groups other than my own?

A publisher:	It will be difficult to put together the perfect Reader. What about classic stories from the past? Will we be restricted to using only contemporary material?
A mother:	I stay at home full-time. I want my children to have positive role models, but will they think less of me because I don't have a glamorous career?
A nonwhite father:	I want my son to be street-proofed. He should know the kinds of attitudes that are out there. But I also don't want him growing up thinking that only white males succeed and have adventures.
A child psychologist:	The absence of positive role models can damage a child's self-esteem. Racist and sexist stereotypes can be internalized and begin to shape a child's behavior.
A civil rights activist:	People's attitudes have to change—education is the key. A simple ban on racism and sexism isn't enough; these images have to be replaced with positive images.

Although there may be other perspectives you can imagine, this list helps illustrate how role-playing works. You can now reexamine your initial decision in the light of multiple views and perhaps opt for a more balanced approach that might appeal to a wider spectrum of concerns. For example, you might decide that the problem is not really the Readers at all, but whether racism and sexism are discussed in the classroom, and, if so, how they are discussed. Or you might decide that an important perspective still missing from the issue is that of children themselves, and you might want to ask some children what they enjoy reading, whether they want to be like the children in their storybooks, or whether the stories ever hurt their feelings.

Remember that generating multiple perspectives is designed to help you move beyond the surface of an issue, so that you can appreciate its complexities. Because most students have been trained to think in terms of right and wrong, recognizing this complexity can seem a bit scary. The role-playing strategy can help you realize that absolutes like right and wrong, although comfortable, are often superficial. You will learn more and push yourself toward better solutions and more creative ideas if you explore the complexities of an issue rather than ignore them.

Shifting Your Own Patterns of Thinking

Perspectives are shaped not only by experience and knowledge, but also by attitudes and moods. When we feel tired, small annoyances sometimes seem like insurmountable problems; but when we are feeling especially cheerful, we are sometimes able to put our problems "into perspective" and so deal with them effectively. Shifting your own patterns of thinking means adopting in a deliberate way a particular attitude or mood that, in turn, will affect your selection, organization, and interpretation of data. Basically, this strategy is a variation on playing the devil's advocate; instead of just adopting the opposite point of view, you can play your hunches and consciously adopt particular attitudes that will help you shift your own patterns of thinking.

Illustration

Suppose that you are asked to write a paper or lead a class discussion evaluating the following statement: "Racism and sexism are much less serious problems in my hometown now than they were in the 1950s." By approaching this statement in four distinct ways, you can begin to practice the kind of flexibility and openness necessary for critical thinking.

Playing Your Hunches

The first step in this strategy is to play your hunches, or listen to your own feelings and instincts about the topic. The goal here is to acknowledge your first reactions and to recognize that your feelings often do shape your perspectives on certain issues. By writing down these initial reactions, you have a better chance of connecting with issues in a personally meaningful way, as well as a better chance of recognizing your biases. Although they should not substitute for evidence, feelings should not be ignored. If you allow yourself the freedom to express your feelings about a topic and label them clearly as such, you are, in a sense, making them visible, so that you can deal with them in a self-conscious way. Feelings, hunches, and instincts can be useful guides in the thinking process and a productive way of becoming motivated. The common view that emotions distort thinking is misleading: it would be more accurate to say that unacknowledged emotions can distort thinking.

Obviously, there can be a wide range of emotional responses to the notion that racism and sexism are in decline. You do not need to justify your feelings to anyone. Merely write them down so that you can look at them; use them to connect with the topic; and temporarily set them aside until you have explored other possibilities. A sample response might be as follows:

> I would like to believe that this statement is true—but deep down I don't believe it is. Sure, there are more opportunities for women and better laws, but some people in my home-town, anyway, are still prejudiced and that's pretty hard to change. I can go along with the idea that maybe there's less sexism—was that even a word in the 1950s? But my instincts tell me that racism is still a problem, and maybe even a worse problem in some ways than it was then.

The Optimistic View

Once you have expressed your initial feelings, you are ready to begin shifting your own patterns of thinking. Quite deliberately and regardless of your instincts, try to think about the statement in a positive and optimistic way. You want to engage in constructive thinking, and consider the kinds of changes and measures you could investigate that would support the idea of improvement in racist and sexist attitudes. The list you make might include some of the following points that you could research:

Employment opportunities
Employment advancement
Better education, higher education, or both
Local action groups—more social awareness
More tolerant immigration policies

Once you allow that there may indeed be positive evidence available to support the statement, you are ready to shift your thinking again.

The Pessimistic View

Now consider the ways in which you can challenge or qualify some of the points on your optimistic list. For example, if you compared the job opportunities available in the 1950s with those available now, you would almost certainly note an improved picture. But would that improvement necessarily mean that society is more tolerant? The demands of an expanding economy may also account for increased job opportunities for women and minorities. Pessimistic thinking can raise doubts and questions about the ways in which racism and sexism can be measured. It can also involve adopting a negative position toward an issue—in which case, you could make a second list of points to research, such as violence against minority groups or equal access to education. Again, the point here is to acknowledge possible problems, complexities, and contradictions in evidence.

Provocative Thinking

So far, by expressing your feelings about the topic and exploring it from a positive and then a skeptical point of view, you have been mapping out relevant perspectives. You have also, perhaps unconsciously, been restricting your thinking to the framework of the statement given to you, with its inherent assumption that levels of racism and sexism can be measured over time. Provocative or lateral thinking invites you to reverse the statement, rethink its framework, or escape that framework altogether. Doing so may help you expand your map of the topic and maybe discover some unexpected perspectives and insights.

For example, would your feelings about the issue shift if the statement were reversed and you were asked to evaluate the notion that racism and sexism in your hometown are now a greater problem than they were in the 1950s? Such a reversal may lead you to think about how to define the nature of problems, instead of concentrating solely on the definitions of racism or sexism.

Alternatively, you might rethink the assumption that you should be looking only for quantitative kinds of evidence, that is, statistics or measurable differences in laws. This assumption stems from the "more-or-less" phrasing of the statement and can be easily challenged. Since a great deal of experience cannot be measured at all, might it be worthwhile to survey the impressions and feelings of some of the people in your hometown about the statement? Should you try to make an argument that people's perceptions about the issue are, in some ways, as valid as hard numbers and graphs?

Finally, consider, for the sake of being provocative, that no one really knows what racism and sexism actually mean. The two words have become so politically loaded that people tend to respond to them in automatic, judgmental ways. Are there any more specific ways of talking about these concepts? Perhaps an interesting point to research might be the ways in which the definitions and contexts of these words have changed since the 1950s.

The value of this four-stage strategy lies not so much in the actual questions or details of information that might occur to you, as in the habit of deliberately shifting your patterns of thinking. The point is that we can see the world through a kaleidoscope, and that, once we do, we will seldom be content with the monocular view and the superficial response.

LEARNING TO FORMULATE AND APPLY QUESTIONS

Many learning strategies provide a framework for asking particular kinds of questions that will help you solve particular problems. Aside from problem solving, however, questioning is vital to generating and developing ideas and to extending understanding. It might even be argued that a college degree represents not just a base of knowledge, but also the ability to construct knowledge by asking questions that gather information, set new problems, and explore abstract concepts. An effective learner is also an effective questioner.

The central role that questioning plays in education is quickly evident when you glance through many college-level textbooks and anthologies. Most contain sets of questions at the end of chapters, sections, or readings—questions designed to help you absorb, focus on, and begin relating particular themes and issues. Working through these questions is good practice, but eventually you will need to be able to pose questions of your own. Critical thinkers actively construct their own questions to connect new information to what they already know and to examine their own thinking process. Undoubtedly, you can learn a great deal from questions provided for you, including some ideas about what kinds of questions are appropriate. However, it is generating your own questions that signals active, independent thinking.

It might seem that asking questions is a simple and even inevitable task. From childhood, we are accustomed to asking questions about all sorts of things. But most of us have also experienced times when we feel reluctant to pose questions, uncertain about what questions to ask, or even unable to think of a question to raise. You may also have experienced the feeling that the answers you receive are not the ones you hoped your questions would elicit, and so you find yourself trying to rephrase or clarify your questions. Part of the art of questioning, then, is to learn a number of questioning strategies and to choose from among them the strategy best suited to a particular situation. For example, if you were to ask your instructor, "What do you want me to write about in this essay?" you would likely receive a somewhat chilly and sketchy response. However, if you explained to the instructor what specific ideas you had already planned on exploring and then asked, "Am I on the right track?" you would probably receive a good deal of helpful advice. Knowing when to ask what questions is an important part of learning.

Of course, not all questions are designed for the same purpose. Some questions are straightforward and intended to gather facts or concrete information. For example, "who," "when," and "where" questions generally elicit fairly brief and specific answers. Questions that begin with "what," "how," and "why" tend to be used to explore abstract concepts, to relate ideas, and to develop them. The questions raised in this category are also often used as problem-setters, and so are starting points for further inquiry. You might ask yourself, "How can I best approach my instructor for help?" and this question, in turn, sets the problem in a particular context that will encourage you to consider your goals more carefully and generate a range of alternatives for achieving them.

While questioning is generally viewed as a positive activity, indicating a curious and engaged mind, you also need to be aware that sometimes questions are used in negative ways—to be evasive or to substitute someone else's thinking for your own. This is likely the conclusion drawn by the instructor who refuses to answer the question, "What do you want me to write about in this essay?" Such a question seems less an attempt at serious inquiry than an effort to discover and adopt wholesale someone else's ideas. At some point in the questioning process, you must take responsibility for formulating your own answers and for being willing to have them evaluated by others. By and large, however, as long as your questions are genuine, you need not fear asking them. The answers you and others provide will help you learn.

Although many of the learning strategies in this book already suggest useful patterns of questions, this section outlines three strategies to help you practice generating and clarifying questions of your own. The strategies are designed to help you deal with three particular situations:

1. Making broad questions more specific
2. Generating questions when you fear you have none
3. Using a checklist of questions to minimize errors in thinking

Making Broad Questions More Specific

Some questions are so huge that they are immediately intimidating, and almost impossible to answer. What do you say when someone asks you to explain who you are? The answer must involve so much information, so much about your experience and beliefs, that often you do not know where to begin. Without intending to do so, many students pose questions for themselves that are so broad that they become far more difficult to answer than they need be. By learning to break down a question into its relevant parts, you may discover that you have more information and more knowledge than you suppose.

Read the very short story, "The Zebra Storyteller," by Spencer Holst. When you have finished, pose for yourself the question, "What does it mean?" Unless you are a very experienced reader, you are likely to find this question too huge to answer. Many students quit trying at this point, convinced that they are not clever enough to formulate an answer or that the story is too trivial to bother trying.

If, however, you redirect your attention to the question itself, you may see ways in which it can be broken down into a series of much more specific questions that you have a much better chance of answering. "What does it mean?" is really a way of asking all at once some of the following questions:

1. What happens in the story?
2. Who are the chief characters?
3. What are the key events or turning points?
4. Are there key details or descriptions that the author emphasizes?
5. What are the key relationships and conflicts in the story?
6. How does the story relate to the course I'm taking or to other stories I've read?

Once the broad question is broken down into more specific questions, you can make a start in formulating an answer. The specific questions pull different kinds of information into focus and allow you a chance to synthesize this information into a possible answer, rather than having to leap to an immediate insight, which you may or may not have. By reviewing who does what, in what order and why, you can begin to play with some possible interpretations—and by rephrasing the question in terms of what the story *might* mean, you free yourself from the pressure of finding some absolute answer. You might also know something about parables already and so be alerted to looking for a moral or a lesson. You might take the point of view of the cat and decide that the story warns us not to pretend to be something we are not. Or you might take the view of the storyteller of the zebras, and speculate that whatever can be imagined is possible. The point is that the starting question becomes manageable when it becomes specific.

Asking questions that are too broad is a common error made by many students. Sadly, when such questions cannot be answered effectively, most students blame themselves instead of reexamining the question.

THE ZEBRA STORYTELLER

Spencer Holst

Once upon a time there was a Siamese cat who pretended to be a lion and spoke inappropriate Zebraic.

That language is whinnied by the race of striped horses in Africa.

Here now: An innocent zebra is walking in a jungle and approaching from another direction is the little cat; they meet.

"Hello there!" says the Siamese cat in perfectly pronounced Zebraic, "It certainly is a pleasant day, isn't it? The sun is shining, the birds are singing, isn't the world a lovely place to live today!"

The zebra is so astonished at hearing a Siamese cat speaking like a zebra, why—he's just fit to be tied.

So the little cat quickly ties him up, kills him, and drags the better parts of the carcass back to his den.

The cat successfully hunted zebras many months in this manner, dining on filet mignon of zebra every night, and from the better hides he made bow neckties and wide belts after the fashion of the decadent princes of the Old Siamese court.

He began boasting to his friends he was a lion, and he gave them as proof the fact that he hunted zebras.

The delicate noses of the zebras told them there was really no lion in the neighborhood. The zebra deaths caused many to avoid the region. Superstitious, they decided the woods were haunted by the ghost of a lion.

One day the storyteller of the zebras was ambling, and through his mind ran plots for stories to amuse the other zebras, when suddenly his eyes brightened, and he said, "That's it! I'll tell a story about a Siamese cat who learns to speak our language! What an idea! That'll make 'em laugh!"

Just then the Siamese cat appeared before him, and said, "Hello there! Pleasant day today, isn't it?"

The zebra storyteller wasn't fit to be tied at hearing a cat speaking his language, because he'd been thinking about that very thing.

He took a good look at the cat, and he didn't know why, but there was something about his looks he didn't like, so he kicked him with a hoof and killed him.

That is the function of the storyteller.

Generating Questions When You Fear You Have None

One of the factors that often prevents us from asking questions is the fear that the question we raise will seem trivial or uninformed to an expert. Although generally questions reveal curiosity and a desire to learn, they also occasionally reveal ignorance, and it is this fear of exposure that keeps us silent. In addition, sometimes we need to have a little prior knowledge about a topic or issue to be able to formulate a question. For example, in the illustration of how to narrow questions that are too broad, it is assumed that you have some prior experience in reading fiction and are aware of some of the categories used to analyze fiction. But what can you do when you know little about a subject and so hesitate or feel unable to raise questions?

An effective strategy for dealing with this kind of situation is to know and test several different types of sequence questions that are general enough to get you started but precise enough to be answerable. One sequence is to examine an issue from past, present, and future perspectives. For example, you might know very little about the complex economic factors that contribute to inflation, but you could ask when the term inflation first began to be used, what its current meaning is, and how this meaning might influence future definitions. By investigating past, present, and future views, you are actually focusing on how definitions and understandings originate and change over time. The focus is general enough to be applied to a wide range of subjects and ideas, yet the information you gather will likely help you generate increasingly informed questions.

A second useful sequence is to ask what comes first, second, third, and so on. When you are faced with very complicated issues, asking these questions is quite reasonable because they will help you order and organize new material. Although in most instances the ordering will be straightforward, sometimes these questions can be used to trigger philosophical and provocative kinds of thinking. For example, in wondering about the functions of a storyteller, an issue raised by Holst's parable, you might ask what comes first—the reality of a cat who speaks the language of the zebras, or the storyteller's imagining of such a cat? Does reality determine imagination, or does imagination determine reality?

A third sequence of questions is to examine a topic, usually a controversial one, using the following series of words: must, should, can't, and shouldn't.[6] This sequence will help you narrow a broad question, such as what can be done about racism and sexism, by examining it from within certain boundaries. The four key words suggest four different modes of thinking, or four different scenarios: *must* suggests urgency, a call for practical and probably short-term action; *should* is more philosophical, inviting speculation about both the need for action and for ideal, and perhaps long-term, policies; *can't* highlights what is impossible to do; and *shouldn't* points to what is undesirable or ill-advised. Phrasing a series of questions around these four words will help you develop an idea and begin to appreciate its complexities. These questions will also help you evaluate your own, as well as any other, solutions offered in response to the problem.

Finally, when you feel you lack the knowledge to formulate a relevant and serious question, you need to try relating the unknown to the known. A simple strategy for doing this is to ask questions that invite both positive and negative comparisons. Instead of asking, "How can a nation allow its debt to become so high?"—a question that may well seem querulous or too vague—you might ask, "How is a nation's debt like my own debts?" and "How is it not like my own debts?" These two more specific questions, which link a complicated economic problem to a common experience, will likely elicit some concrete examples that will help you better understand the larger issue.

Positive and negative comparison questions can also help you develop your lateral thinking and can be used to challenge definitions or concepts. After reading "The Zebra Storyteller," you might ask: "How is a story like reality?" "How is it not like reality?" "Why is life stranger than fiction?" "Why is it not?" Although these kinds of ques-

6. Rob Barnes, *Successful Study for Degrees* (London: Routledge, 1992) 44.

tions might not have definite answers, they will enable you to extend your ideas and to participate fully in discussions.

Using Questions to Minimize Errors in Thinking

Critical thinkers ask questions of themselves, not just of others. Self-questioning makes us more aware of our thinking patterns and also helps us evaluate our ideas. Many students find it useful to have a personal checklist of questions designed to minimize errors they might tend to make in their thinking. Two very common errors in thinking are overlooking a crucial variable or piece of information and assuming that any answers we have worked out must be right. To lessen the effects of these errors, you can check your thinking periodically with these two questions: "Is there more to this problem, issue, or situation than I am currently seeing?" and "Have I fairly considered other views or tried to generate alternatives?"

For your checklist to be truly effective, you need to generate your own questions, because, as a critical thinker, you will know your own thinking patterns better than anyone else. To begin your list, however, you might want to think about any recurring questions you are in the habit of asking. For example, if you often ask yourself how to get started, you may have a problem with motivation. Try leading off your checklist with a question that will help you make personal connections to the material you are studying, such as "What am I most curious about regarding this issue, story, or assignment?" or "How can I connect this issue to my own experience?" As you gain practice in thinking critically, you can add to, or revise your list, but avoid making it too long. You want a quick check, not an exhaustive inquisition.

Finally, remember that you are asking questions in a particular frame of reference: an academic discipline in a college, where inquiry and the advancement of inquiry are crucial aims. Think about the kinds of questions being asked by the instructors in any given subject area—the questions are often more important than the answers.

DEVELOPING FRAMEWORKS FOR CRITICAL THINKING

An important aspect of any critical thinking activity is to be self-conscious about, or aware of, the mental pathways we are following. Most of us, however, do not think about how we think. Thinking is like breathing: an automatic and internalized process, which is not visible and therefore difficult to explain. To demystify the thinking process and to develop and focus it, we need to make this implicit process explicit. In other words, we need to be able to visualize thinking patterns.

Developing frameworks for critical thinking in a specific academic discipline is one method of mapping, or visualizing, the complex task of analysis. Often, this task is neither made explicit nor broken down into stages for students simply because the expert thinkers in the discipline now analyze material almost automatically. As a result, the novice views analysis itself as a difficult task or a gift, rather than as a skill that can be learned, practiced, and improved. Frameworks for critical thinking necessarily simplify the analytical process, but they can provide a starting point for building skills. By making explicit some of the activities that expert thinkers engage in, frameworks function as models, prompting certain questions, introducing important categories, and helping us become more aware of what we do when we think.

Most frameworks for critical thinking are developed around implicit questions. Are there core issues or concepts that recur in your thinking about a particular subject area? What information do you begin with, and how can you build on this information to move from description to analysis? The sample frameworks offered in this section attempt to answer some of these questions and to map out either specific activities or perspectives.

The frameworks themselves are not intended to be rigid: feel free to amend them and experiment with them. As frameworks, they can model certain kinds of thinking or approaches to thinking, but they do not provide rules for thinking. You need to guide or direct your thinking along certain paths in order to be analytical, but you do not want to be so rule-bound that you negate the possibilities for creativity and insight.

A General or Thematic Model

This framework for critical thinking can be adapted to different kinds of subject areas or to themes being studied in particular courses. It lays out, almost in the manner of a mathematical formula, a series of categories to consider in the movement from description to analysis:

Concrete Descriptions + Category of Text + Variables from the course of Study + Context + Author's Possible Intentions = Analysis[7]

When you describe something, you are merely stating or listing its features, as in retelling the plot of a story. Analysis, on the other hand

---

7. Adapted from a model discussed by Chet Meyers, *Teaching Students to Think Critically* (San Francisco: Jossey-Bass, 1986) 7–8.

(even though it can have slightly different meanings, depending on the academic field of study), generally requires you to assign significance ✓ to something. In other words, you need to think critically about its parts, the relationship among parts, the validity of its parts, and so on. By applying this framework to Thurber's story, "The Rabbits Who Caused All The Trouble," it is possible to map the movement from description to analysis. Let us also suppose that this story is being read for a college composition course.

Illustration

Concrete Descriptions

The first stage of the framework is to begin with what you know or with what you have been given. You can jot down a quick summary of the plot:

> A group of wolves, who dislike rabbits, threaten and then destroy them. The rabbits don't run because they believe the other animals will protect them and because they do not wish to seem cowardly. The other animals, however, prove to be ineffectual.

Besides summarizing the plot you might list any vivid descriptions and any patterns of repetition used in the story. For example, you might note that the wolves call the rabbits names, blame them for natural disasters, such as earthquakes and floods, and echo the words of the other animals when called on by them to justify their treatment of the rabbits.

At this initial stage, you are not interpreting but merely noting and observing the details of the story. As you continue to work through the framework, you may return to this stage at any point, adding details and looking for textual evidence to support your analysis of the story.

Category of Text

This part of the framework focuses attention on the kind of material you are analyzing. A "text" can take many forms: it can be a painting, a building, a newspaper article, a historical document, a novel, a speech, and so on. In this instance, Thurber's story belongs to a category of fiction known as a fable. Write down anything you know about fables, or look up "fable" in a dictionary to see if the definition offers any clues that can help you formulate an analytical response to the story.

You will discover that a fable is a short tale that is often told to teach a moral and frequently has animals as characters. Sometimes, a fable is defined as a story about supernatural or extraordinary persons or events, and sometimes as a story not founded on fact. This information will direct your attention to Thurber's stated moral, and it might prompt you to think about other useful questions. Is the moral at all surprising in the light of other fables you might have read? Could there be a specific reason for Thurber's choice of this particular form? Do the animals have human counterparts, and, if so, what are they? Explore this part of the framework for as long as it helps you to generate questions or ideas, and then move on to the next. You will be carrying over information from one part of the framework to the next, so you need not feel you are abandoning anything you may have discovered.

Variables from the Course of Study

Variables are the major ideas, concepts, and theories being taught in a given course. They can help you understand a reading from a particular academic perspective and situate a particular text in the larger framework of a theme or course. Suppose that this reading is assigned in a college composition course within the section on argument and persuasion. You can use this information to raise some questions specific to the course: "What do you think Thurber is trying to argue?" and "Why has he chosen to use humor as a persuasive technique?" You might even notice that Thurber uses deliberately flawed arguments (those given by the wolves and the other animals) in order to make his larger argument.

No doubt, variables will change as courses progress or change, so this is a part of the critical thinking framework that you must always revise and update. You can also consider other assigned texts as variables in a course and compare Thurber's argumentative strategies with those of other authors. As noted earlier, comparing Thurber's moral with the morals typical of other fables can be an instructive exercise. If you have any trouble deciding on what variables to use, ask some of your classmates to list what they see as the main theories or concepts of a course or theme. You can also show a tentative list to your teacher and ask for feedback.

Because this part of the framework for critical thinking directs your attention to the intellectual content of a course, it is a valuable aid in enhancing comprehension. It can also serve you well in reviewing material.

Context

Thurber was an American humorist who wrote this fable in 1955. He was also a journalist, cartoonist, and a managing editor of *The New*

Yorker. At the context stage of the critical thinking framework, you should speculate as to how this information about historical time and place might provide some useful insights into the significance of the fable and its moral.

In 1955, the world was in the midst of the Cold War. The United Nations was being tested in its resolve to contain and control aggression. The Korean War had ended, and Eastern Europe was sorting out political chaos in the aftermath of the Second World War. Added to this context is the similarity between political language in the journalism of the time and the language used by Thurber in the fable. For example, the wolves, who are clearly the aggressors in the tale, attempt to disguise their intentions by talking about "civilizing" the rabbits and about "imprisoning" them "for their own protection." When challenged by the other animals to account for their actions, they claim that the matter is a purely "internal" one. Once you make a connection between politics and the fable it is irresistible to see the other animals as representative of the United Nations and the rabbits as any number of small countries or minority groups faced with the prejudice and aggression of more powerful countries represented by the wolves.

At this point, you have moved well beyond description and clearly have an analytical view of the story. However, you will want to test your ideas about the story's possible meaning by going back to the earlier stages of the framework, looking for supporting textual evidence in the language and dramatic events of the fable, and fitting in other pieces of information that you may have gathered. You may even want to read some more of Thurber's fiction to see if this kind of humorous political commentary is typical of his writing.

Author's Possible Intentions

This part of the model is carefully pluralized to help you avoid making an error in thinking called the intentional fallacy. Even though it is possible to make a reasonable guess as to what Thurber intended to communicate in his fable, it would be unwise to assume that he, or any other author, *must* have intended only one meaning. It is more productive for you to suspend judgment and consider a range of possible intentions. For example, you have enough textual evidence to argue that Thurber is, indeed, making a political observation in tune with the events of the time, but it would be very hasty to assume that the fable was specifically about North and South Korea or about Hungary and Russia. In fact, since fables are often about human foibles and typical behavior, you could even argue that his story becomes timeless and is as relevant today as it was in 1955.

Thurber's other intentions might include an indirect criticism of the United Nations or of the gullibility of the rabbits, who too quickly believe that others will save them. Given the irony and humor of the moral, Thurber may also be inviting readers to reexamine their own assumptions and values about when to fight and when to run. Finally, and not insignificantly, Thurber is demonstrating his own ingenuity by taking what seems an old-fashioned form often reserved for children and using it to help adults recognize their own folly in contemporary affairs.

Each part of the critical thinking framework prompts you to think about the fable in a new way and gradually build your own interpretation. As you gain practice in applying the framework, you will be able to adapt it to specific academic disciplines. For example, if the text you are asked to analyze is a painting, you might list colors or images under concrete descriptions; if it is a government document, you might list facts and statistical information and think about the source and purpose of that information. There is nothing magical about the framework itself—after all, you are still the person doing the thinking. But the model may help you direct your thinking in productive ways and give you a structure for gathering and interrelating ideas.

Modes of Perception in Literature

The model we turn to now is a framework for critical thinking about literature adapted from Carol Holmberg, who wanted to give her students a visual model of different ways of perceiving and interpreting fictional material.[8] As in the previous model, you can move through each of the four stages, shifting the ways in which you are thinking about literature and so gradually moving from description to analysis. Holmberg uses visual metaphor, that of an expanding lens, to illustrate expanding perceptions. However, you can also think about the following four modes of perception as rungs on a ladder that you climb in reaching an analytical interpretation:

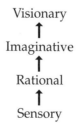

Visionary
↑
Imaginative
↑
Rational
↑
Sensory

8. Discussed in Meyers 18–20.

You can begin working with this model by applying it to Holst's "The Zebra Storyteller."

Illustration

Sensory Level

As in the general or thematic model, your perceptions of the story usually start at the sensory or concrete level, so here you will note the basic images and story line of Holst's tale. On a concrete or descriptive level, you might say that the story is about a Siamese cat, who so surprises the zebras by learning their language that he is able to overpower them and gain a reputation as a great hunter. He boasts that he is a lion, and even the zebras begin to believe in a superstitious notion of a lion's ghost. The zebra storyteller, however, imagines a cat able to speak Zebraic and so is not surprised when the Siamese cat approaches him. His suspicions aroused, the storyteller kills the cat. On a literal level, this is a good summary of the story. Now you will need to consider the story from different perspectives in order to explore some of its deeper meanings.

Rational Level

Take the information you have gathered at the sensory level and consider it from a rational, or conceptual, perspective. You will be rephrasing the concrete summary in more abstract terms. For example, on a rational level, you might say that the story is about a cat who uses language to trick the zebras until the storyteller uses his imagination to defeat him. Or you might say that the function of the storyteller is to match wits with the enemy or to expect the unexpected. At the rational level, it is important to begin thinking about what the concrete details mean, or what the story is about in a general, thematic sense.

Imaginative Level

To consider the story from an imaginative or metaphorical perspective means that you can begin playing with ideas about what the story's details and theme might represent. Having thought about the details of the story and pondered their meaning, you are now ready to think about the possible significance of the story.

Like Thurber in his fable, Holst uses animal characters and extraordinary events to suggest an analogy to human behavior. His moral is implied in the cryptic closing statement: "That is the function of the storyteller." On a literal, or concrete, level, this function is the killing of the cat, an interpretation that is obviously too narrow to apply very usefully to storytellers in general. To fully appreciate Holst's tale, you need to think about the storyteller's function in metaphorical terms. Perhaps the storyteller is too wise to be tricked, and thus the implied moral might be that you cannot fool all the zebras all of the time. More in keeping with the details of the story, however, is the connection between language, power, and imagination. The function of the storyteller might be to anticipate the unimaginable or to stretch the limits of imagination and possibility.

Visionary Level

As you have moved up the ladder toward higher levels of analysis, your sense of what Holst's story is saying has been expanding. This final level invites you to explore any philosophical, mythic, or universal statements Holst may be implying in the telling of his tale. After all, he too is a storyteller, and perhaps we are like the zebras who place too much trust in what is reasonable and so cannot respond to the miraculous. It is possible that Holst is playing with the fine boundary line between reason and imagination or between reality and fiction. These provocative and visionary ideas can become the basis of an original argument, which you can ground in the concrete detail of the text, and which you can explain to others by taking them through the different levels of interpretation.

Frameworks for critical thinking can be very stimulating, but they require some patience in learning and practice in applying. You might want to try using this strategy the first few times with two or three classmates. In that way, you can pool information and become more accustomed to how a framework can be applied before using it on your own. Finally, remember that no matter what the particular design of a critical thinking model may be, the key point is to demystify the process of analysis: to make visible and concrete some of the pathways that the active mind can explore in seeking deeper and richer levels of meaning and interpretation.

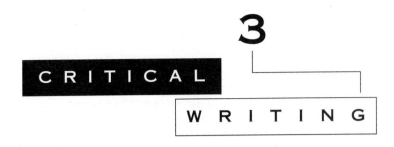

3

CRITICAL

WRITING

DEFINING SUBJECT AND PURPOSE

As you begin to apply the practical strategies in this handbook to your own college courses, you will see that critical reading, thinking, and writing are interrelated and overlapping activities. For example, reading strategies that help you focus on a writer's purpose are likely, when you are writing, to make you more conscious of the need to articulate a purpose of your own. Similarly, learning to think critically about an author's assumptions will help you recognize assumptions in your own writing, and writing of all kinds is a powerful tool for organizing and clarifying your thinking.

When you are learning how to write at the college level, you will probably be exposed to different theories of how people write—theories that divide the composing process into several stages. For example, you may learn that composing is a matter of prewriting, writing, and rewriting, or of generating and planning, drafting, and revising. The advantage of dividing the writing process is that each stage helps you concentrate on specific activities and so gain more control of the overall process. The disadvantage is that you are likely to view each stage as discrete and the process itself as linear. In other words, it is easy to assume that once you have completed one step in the process you are ready for the next and, if you are a good writer, do not need to return to an earlier step.

Expert writers testify, however, that writing is far messier than this neat and progressive model suggests. Although the composing process can be divided into different stages, it is crucial to remember that the stages often overlap and that the process is recursive: the activity of writing a first draft often triggers new ideas, causing you to return to the earlier stages of generating and planning. Similarly, revising, which is often viewed as a final step, is actually a creative activity that occurs throughout the process, whenever you are rethinking your approach to a particular subject. A recursive process, then, is one in which certain activities recur and are necessarily repeated. Since goals in writing are seldom achieved by marching steadily toward them in a straight line, it is more productive to think of yourself as dancing toward those goals with a choreography that includes moving forward and backward, repeating certain steps, turning around, and turning back.

Each new writing assignment requires a slightly new choreography, and no two writers are likely to have the same one. Thus, expert writers come to recognize the complexity of writing as an inherent part of the process, and they learn specific strategies to deal with problems as they occur and recur. Novice writers are more likely to view the messiness of the process as a kind of personal inadequacy and so abandon the dance just when it is becoming interesting. Part of learning to write critically, then, is to be aware of the composing process and, as in reading or thinking critically, be able to apply practical strategies that help in coping with its complexities.

Writing at the college level also entails dealing with special pressures dictated by an academic setting. The fact that at some point your writing will be graded is a large part of this pressure. You may also feel intimidated about writing for a primary reader (your instructor) who obviously knows more about a given subject than you do. If you are taking several courses, you may well have several essays due at the same time. Finally, you may believe that you can safely say only what you think the instructor wants to hear and so have little faith in the process of generating your own ideas. All of these pressures are certainly real enough, and it is better to try to confront them than to ignore them.

Part of your responsibility as a critical writer is to begin to think of writing as an opportunity for learning and for communicating your ideas to others. This well-worn advice may sound corny and overly idealistic to you. Nevertheless, it expresses the motivation most people have for any kind of writing they do—notes to friends, lists, memos, personal diary entries, and so on. Writing helps us clarify and organize our thoughts, and it helps us influence other people by expressing our ideas and feelings. These ways of thinking about writing should not be abandoned just because it is necessary to write for a grade.

There are ways to manage the stress associated with academic writing. You can learn to use your time more efficiently. You can also imagine and write to a reader less intimidating than your instructor. As you gain experience in generating ideas, you will be more excited and more confident about expressing them. The point is that most of the pressures surrounding the act of writing in college, including lack of confidence, can be reduced if you look at them from a fresh perspective and learn strategies for confronting them.

Probably, by the time you enter college, you will already have developed certain habits in regard to writing. It is important for you to think about what you do when you write and why you do it. Becoming aware of the activities you engage in can help you sort out what works well for you, what skills you may need to develop, and what rules or myths need to be dismissed. Perhaps the most alluring myth of all is the belief that you can become inspired at the last moment, write an essay the night before, fix up a word here and there, and receive an A. This myth persists because we all have met people who claim to have done exactly this. In the odd magical moment, you may even believe you have done this yourself. Most likely, however, the single-draft writer actually did some very serious and intense thinking before starting to write and had mentally revised different ideas and approaches several times before expressing them on paper. Different writers write in different ways, but inspiration is hard work despite the appearance of ease. Although you can learn how to make the work you do more productive, there is no substitution for the work itself. Still, you can take comfort from knowing that everyone else has to do the work, too.

The strategies in this section are designed to help you define a subject and purpose for writing assignments. They are especially useful when you are beginning to compose, but because the process is recursive, you may want to reapply them several times throughout the writing of an essay. These strategies can also help you generate ideas and plan and organize a draft.

Defining Subject and Purpose

DESIRE ON DOMINO ISLAND
Lee Smith

Preface

Some summers back, my friend Katherine Kearns, who was pregnant and bored at the time, decided that she wanted to write a romance novel. So she sent off to Silhouette Romances for guidelines, temporarily abandoned her pursuit of the Ph.D. in English at the University of North Carolina, and set to work.

Some of the guidelines follow:

Our Heroine is, preferably, an orphan. She is alone in the world. (Note: A brother is, in some cases, permissible, but only if he is retarded or has not found his way in life.) Our heroine appears frail, but looks terrific when she gets dressed up. She is, of course, a virgin. She arrives alone in the lush romantic Setting, where she encounters our Hero, who is preferably dark, brooding, and mysterious (although we have had some luck recently with stern Nordic sorts and hunky redheads). The initial encounter is tempestuous. Sparks fly, yet there is of course a mad underlying attraction. The Other Woman will be beautiful, desirable, and wealthy. She is, of course, a bitch. The Other Man will be nice, boring, well-meaning, intent upon saving our Heroine from the clutches of our Hero and the dangerous contingencies of the Plot. (Note: No other main characters will be permitted in this novel, *especially children*. Any necessary others, such as a faithful housekeeper, should remain as stereotypical as possible, so as not to detract from the romance.) The Plot will ensue, with the ten chapters growing increasingly shorter as tension mounts. At the climax, our Hero and Heroine realize that they are made for each other after all. The novel ends with their passionate embrace. (Note: At no time during this novel will they or anyone else ever actually *do it*, nor will any specific body parts be mentioned.)

My friend Katherine did not sell her novel to Silhouette Romances, even though she came up with a wonderful heroine who inherited an old inn on Pawley's Island, South Carolina, and a mysterious saturnine artist who painted there. Her novel, *A Certain Slant of Light*, turned out to have two qualities that are not permissible: symbolism, and semicolons. But I, still intrigued by the guidelines, wrote this Silhouette Romance.

Chapter One

As the sleek motorboat slices through the aqua effervescence of Domino Bay to approach the pearly brightness of the beach, Jennifer surveys the lush scene before her with no small trepidation, and a hint of dismay creeps into her normally dulcet tone as she exclaims, "Captain! Oh, Captain! Why are you docking here in the middle of nowhere? Is there no settlement of any sort hereabouts? I had expected . . ."

But the captain won't say a thing! A native Georgian with an unfortunately cleft palate, he shoots a dark glance from beneath his surly brow at the clearly frightened young woman and mumbles something indistinguishable into his dark facial hair. He throws her bags on the beach. He heaves his bulk around.

Jennifer drums her small fingers rat-a-tat-tat on the hull of the shiny craft. Is it all a huge mistake, her coming here? But what else could she have done, considering the terrible fire that swept the home of her guardians (since their parents' mysterious death some twenty years ago, Jennifer and her retarded brother, Lewis, have been most carefully raised), killing both Aunt Lucia and Uncle Norm and destroying the entire perfect loveliness of their antebellum mansion, leaving Jennifer with only her small inheritance, her paltry background in microbiology, and the hunting lodge somewhere deep within the fastnesses of this fabled island.

"I had hoped . . ." But Jennifer's words are lost in the slap of the waves and the oddly shrill cries of the brilliant birds that wheel in the hot blue sky. Parrots and shy tropical creatures peek out at her from the shiny green leaves of the junglelike vegetation which threatens to engulf the beach; the shriek of an apparent panther is heard.

"Harg!" the captain barks. Clearly he wants to be quit of this spot before dark, wants to be back on the mainland hefting a brew with his rustic buddies.

Jennifer mounts the dock with a sigh, traverses its rotting length, and turns to wave a reluctant farewell to the enigmatic captain, who even now is rounding the great Grey Lady rocks which mark the harbor, slipping from her view. Well.

Although she is petite and somewhat fragile in appearance, a spark of mischief in Jennifer's eye belies the seeming frailty of her frame. Actually Jennifer is not frail at all! She's as strong as an ox, and also she looks terrific when she gets dressed up. But right now she wears a lime-green T-shirt, a khaki wrap-around skirt, and espadrilles. Her wispy brown locks are caught fast in a gold barrette which used to belong to her mother. Jennifer hoists the weight of her luggage and trudges through the wet unwelcoming sand across the narrow beach and up the faint trail into the very jungle, vines slowing her progress as she bites her lip to hold back her brimming tears, as night begins to fall. . . .

Chapter Two

Plucky Jennifer manages to set up her tent in a clearing beneath a giant live oak, where she eats a granola bar, lights her Coleman lantern, and soon is competently ensconced in the jungle wilderness.

But suddenly we note the rustle of palm fronds, the swish of savannah grass, the warning chorus of tree frogs. Footsteps are heard on the path. Jennifer, who was very nearly asleep, stands to face the invader. Jennifer's teeth clatter helplessly in the tropic night.

"Yes?" she cries bravely into the darkness. "Yes? Who's there?"

"Rock Cliff," comes the terse reply.

"I don't believe I have had the pleasure!" Jennifer casts open the tent fly.

Light streams out to reveal the rugged virile form clad in well-worn (tight) blue jeans, cowboy boots, and an old torn Brooks Brothers shirt open almost to the waist, unveiling the wealth of dark hair on the broad, muscled chest. Beneath the sable sweep of unruly hair and the decisive black line of his eyebrows, Rock Cliff's dark eyes flash fire above the prominent jut of his cheekbones. There is a touch of world-weariness in the little lines that web the marble wideness of his brow, a suggestion of tenderness and compassion which is offset by the fleshy cruel sensuality of his mouth, his strong white teeth. All his muscles bulge.

Now we are getting somewhere!

"Miss Jennifer Maidenfern?" he inquires rudely in deep masculine tones which send an unwonted tingle up Jennifer's spine.

"I beg your pardon!" she rejoins tartly.

"I received a communication from a Miss Jennifer Maidenfern not long ago, insisting that I vacate immediately the premises of Domino Lodge, where I have been in residence for the past ten months while finishing my novel," Rock Cliff continues. "I have now vacated those premises at enormous psychological cost, as I now find I am unable to complete my novel in any other surroundings. I urge you to reconsider."

It all comes back to Jennifer now. "I sent a letter to the occupant . . ." she says slowly.

"I am the occupant," states Rock Cliff.

"I see." Jennifer realizes she is in danger of losing herself in the fiery depths of his eyes. "I'm terribly sorry," she says with an effort, "but that's quite impossible. I intend to stay."

"I am independently wealthy, " asserts Rock Cliff. "I will pay any amount of money to purchase Domino Lodge." There's a sudden unaccustomed tremor in his voice now and we can tell how much this means to him, how his life of rich playboy decadence has left him empty and unfulfilled, how the completion of this novel will bring back his faith in himself.

Jennifer presses her trembling lips into a firm line. "Goodbye, Mr. Cliff," she says. Attempting with shaking fingers to refasten the tent fly, she stumbles over a tortoise and falls backward suddenly, upsetting the lantern. The ever-alert Rock Cliff springs forward into the tent. Quickly he lunges past the terrified young woman to right the lantern and finds himself there suddenly on the tent floor beside her shy vulnerability and sweet trembling lips which he cannot help but cover with his own. The tent fly drops silently behind him.

So I can't see a damn thing! I want to be in that tent; I want to see it all. I want to know where he puts his hands. But here I am, reading, and there they are inside that tent, black opaque shadows moving against the flap, moving and thrashing and moving until at last he emerges with a muttered oath and stumbles off into the night.

Chapters Three, Four, and Five

are a drag. Nothing much happening here except that Jennifer finally finds Domino Lodge (after several wrong turns, lots of boring flora on the trail) and meets faithful Irish housekeeper Mrs. O'Reilly, an amusing old alcoholic fond of misquoting familiar sayings, as in "Don't put all your eggs under a basset," page 62. Mrs. O'Reilly takes a liking to Jennifer right away, fixing her a hot buttered rum, some scones, some fig preserves. Jennifer eats with interest. Mrs. O'Reilly explains the blood feud which has always existed between the Maidenfern family and the deRigeurs on the other side of the island: an insult, a slight, a missing emerald. Mrs O'Reilly praises the exemplary conduct of the recent occupant Mr. Cliff (Ha! Ha!), relates the complete history of Domino Island, and is working up to its geographic configurations when thank God she is interrupted by the surprise entrance of Charles Fine, the young Episcopal rector from the mainland, who has sailed over in his lovely sloop *The Dove* especially to bid Jennifer welcome.

"Welcome." He smiles.

"Why, thank you," Jennifer returns.

Jennifer cannot fail to notice this young bachelor's peaches-'n'-cream complexion, his lithe body, the warm sincerity of his soft blue gaze.

"If there is anything I can do to assist you," Charles Fine offers as he prepares to cast off, "anything at all . . ." His voice rings like a bell.

"I'll let you know," responds Jennifer. She watches him sail away until his boat is a mere black dot against the shimmering sea; she approves of him, Jennifer does, with all her fluttering heart, and cannot understand the recent blush that climbed her features unawares when Mrs. O'Reilly mentioned that blackguard Rock Cliff. Oh! A hand flies up to Jennifer's mouth. It is, of course, her own.

Chapter Six

So Jennifer settles in. The island sun paints a glint of gold on her plain brown locks and a dusting of freckles across the bridge of her nose. One morning she's hard at work refurbishing all the furniture in the east parlor when who should arrive but Rock Cliff! Jennifer—caught barefooted, no makeup, in one of her oldest frocks—tries to flee the parlor, but he blocks her way with his muscled girth.

"Not so fast, young lady!" drawls Rock Cliff. He actually appears to be amused; how dare he? "I've been thinking it over, and I feel I owe you an apology."

"I should say so!" snaps Jennifer. And then somehow she finds herself weakening, smiling up into those eyes. She can feel his breath on her skin. He leans down closer, closer, closer. . . .

Breaking free with a momentous exercise of pure will, Jennifer evades the virile visitor and commences to wash the woodwork on the other side of the room.

"Now Jennifer," he entreats, following her slim figure. "I want to make it up to you, Jennifer, if I may call you that. I'd like to take you out to dinner tonight."

Furiously, silently, Jennifer scrubs.

Rock Cliff edges even closer. "Come on now," he implores. "I feel a real connection between us, Jennifer. I sensed it from the first. I'm sorry I lost my head, but your nearness combined with the hot charm of the night . . ." Rock Cliff has edged so close to Jennifer that she has been forced to retreat still further, has in fact climbed upon the windowsill itself, a precarious perch.

"Please, my dear," he begs passionately.

"I'm warning you, Rock Cliff!" shrills Jennifer, but then she tumbles—scrub brush, water pail, and all—straight onto the wide-planked cypress floor, overturning a handsome old desk, an ottoman, and Rock Cliff himself, who sprawls violently beside her in the sudden sea of suds.

Jennifer giggles infectiously. Rock Cliff catches her merriment and guffaws heartily, then turns to her with yearning eyes and clasps her wet torso firmly in his rippling arms. "My dear," he says.

"Oh, Rock," yields Jennifer, as . . .

Chapter Seven

"I might have known!" cries Monica deRigeur. "Look at you, Rock Cliff, down there on the floor all wet and unkempt in a compromising position!"

"Now wait just a minute," drawls Rock.

But Jennifer sees the emerald engagement ring on Monica's tapered digit.

"No!" Jennifer leaps up and stamps her petite foot. "Don't wait at all! Just leave! Both of you! I see right through you, Rock Cliff, you and your fashionable fiancée!"

Monica, by the way, is a real bitch wearing a low-necked blue-flowered voile dress which does nothing to hide her voluptuous form.

White high-heeled sandals and a strand of priceless pearls about her swan-like neck complete the ensemble. Her upswept coiffure is elegant, implicit, or imminent, or something. I give up. "Move it, lover boy," she directs haughtily.

"This is all a terrible misunderstanding," Rock states, but the force of Jennifer's grief ejaculates them both from the room.

Chapter Eight

Jennifer sends for her retarded brother and adopts a wild raccoon which she names Bruce, then nicknames Posy.(?)

Chapter Nine

Jennifer and Lewis are sunbathing on the secluded pink shell beach when here comes Charles Fine in his nautically white sloop, ready to propose to Jennifer. "I need a helpmeet," he explains earnestly, holding Jennifer tight in his strong ecclesiastical arms where she sheds a single tear upon realizing who it is she really loves.

"The cat is out of the bag now, I guess!" and, oh no, it's Rock Cliff who has been concealed behind some hydrangea bushes observing this tender scene. Rock Cliff's statement about the cat confuses Lewis, who becomes quite frightened and begins to weep openly. As Jennifer rushes to comfort her poor brother, helpful Charles Fine attempts to explain things to the irate Rock Cliff.

"You must not misconstrue . . ." Charles Fine begins.

"Misconstrue, hell!" shouts Rock Cliff, his fiery temper erupting totally since he has just broken his long-standing engagement to the beauteous Monica deRigeur only to find his dream girl in the arms of another man. Rock Cliff stalks off into the jungle just as lightning splits the summer sky and thunder rolls off the horizon, signaling the oncoming hurricane. A distraught Jennifer resists the fervent pleas of Charles Fine and Mrs. O'Reilly. She insists upon setting off immediately in search of Rock Cliff, and there she goes, accompanied only by her pet raccoon, into the dark wild jungle, into the eye of the storm.

Chapter Ten

just goes on and on! Jennifer is lost in the swamp, buffeted by the hurricane, set upon by wild dogs, defended by Posy, and drenched to the skin. Night falls. Jennifer finally takes shelter in a cave which strangely enough turns out to contain her parents' grave (!) as well as a sealed cask holding some long complicated To Whom It May Concern letter implicating the deRigeurs in her parents' death and explaining the curse of the emerald. *Who cares?* Jennifer tosses and turns in a restless doze yet feels strangely warm because of her parents' presence. At the first blush of dawn she sallies forth and retraces her steps through the jungle until she spots Domino Lodge at last through the dense fronds.

"Posy, we're home!" Jennifer tells the exhausted raccoon.

"And it's about time!" cries Rock Cliff, who has thought better of his hasty actions and has been scouring the jungle all night long for Jennifer. The bedraggled lovers rush toward each other and meet in a passionate embrace on the pink shell beach. Their clothes are all torn and wet, revealing their contours anew in the paleness of dawn. They kiss hungrily as Mrs. O'Reilly, Lewis, and Charles Fine steal out to the edge of the beach to share this happy moment. "Well, it's an ill wind which blows nobody," Mrs. O'Reilly observes with a chuckle, and Charles Fine reveals that he plans to teach Lewis to sail. Rock Cliff casts the unlucky emerald into the waiting waves; Monica deRigeur flies past in her private plane, bound for New York; Posy heaves a sigh of relief; and again the lovers embrace as, behind them, the sun rises out of the sea.

And that's it! I shade my eyes against the brightness of this sun, the glare off the water, but in vain: all I can see is the silhouette. Jennifer and Rock have nothing, nothing left—no faces, no bodies, not to mention fear or pain or children, joy or memory or loss—nothing but these flat black shapes against the tropic sky.

In most cases, the subject of an essay is provided for you by the essay assignment or question. Sometimes, the subject is obvious and quite narrowly defined, as in this assignment: "Discuss how Lee Smith uses form and structure in 'Desire on Domino Island' to parody romance novels." Sometimes, the subject area is given in much broader or more general terms, for instance, "Discuss the phenomenon of the romance novel in popular culture." At other times, the general subject area cannot even be sketched in until you first answer a framing question. In most cases, framing questions are based on a reading or a quotation, as in the following example:

> "I shade my eyes against the brightness of this sun, the glare off the water, but in vain: all I can see is the silhouette. Jennifer and Rock have nothing, nothing left—no faces, no bodies, not to mention fear or pain or children, joy or

memory or loss—nothing but these flat black shapes against the tropic sky."

What is the criticism implied by Lee Smith's final paragraph of "Desire on Domino Island"? Apply this criticism to any romance novel of your choice.

The responsibility of determining a subject may also be completely shifted to you, as in the phrase: "Choose your own topic."

Except for the initial assignment, in which it is clear that the subject of the essay will be how Smith uses form and structure to parody romance novels, you will need to make some choices about the subject and begin narrowing the subject area. Issues or themes discussed in your course, as well as the length requirement of the essay, can guide you in determining and restricting a subject. For example, in a five- or six-page essay, you can hardly say more than the most obvious about the phenomenon of romance novels unless you choose a particular focus. If the assignment is given to you in a course on gender roles, you could choose to focus on images of masculinity in romance novels or on the ways in which sexuality is depicted. If the course is about the values of contemporary society, you might want to explore how the novels define the concept of romance itself; or you might choose as your subject the mass marketing of the novels. No matter what kind of writing assignment you are asked to do, it is vital that you define that subject in terms that are relevant to you, to the question being asked, and to the course being taught.

To determine the purpose of an essay, you need to consider the reasons why you are writing. Thinking about your purposes will help you identify specific issues linked to a subject, clarify your own attitude to the subject, and anticipate the needs of your reader. For example, if you have decided to investigate the marketing of romance novels, you will have to tell your reader what some of the marketing techniques are and also make clear why knowing about this aspect of romance novels is important. Generally, the intellectual framework of the course you are taking can help you determine a primary purpose. In a course about the values of contemporary society, the marketing of romance novels can be a specific and convincing example of consumerism, or of how human desires are subverted by a steady supply of material goods. Determining the purpose of an essay is often a challenging task; look for a larger issue connected to or suggested by the subject. Often, the purpose you define will give the subject context and help the reader understand why you are talking about the subject in the first place.

Determining a subject and purpose that are relevant to the course, interesting to you as a writer, and accessible and engaging to a reader is one of the most important aspects of writing. Accordingly, it is worthwhile to take some time to consider how you might choose or restrict a subject, why you are exploring it, and how you can communicate it most effectively to your reader. The strategies of taking inventory and planning what and how, adapted from Linda Flower's *Problem-Solving Strategies for Writing*, can help you start.[1]

Taking Inventory

This strategy, developed by Linda Flower, author of *Problem-Solving Strategies for Writing*, centers on three questions:

1. What do I know about the subject?
2. What is my attitude toward the subject?
3. What do I want to convince my reader of?

These questions can be asked in any order. They will help you retrieve and survey information you already have about a subject and determine what information you will need to find to develop your subject. Given the nature of the questions, however, this strategy can also help you restrict a subject and determine a purpose for writing.

Illustration

Suppose that you have been asked to write an essay in response to the following two-part assignment: "What criticism is implied by Lee Smith's final paragraph of 'Desire on Domino Island'? Apply this criticism to any romance novel of your choice." To begin thinking about the subject, you must first determine an answer to the framing question. Smith's final paragraph can have several valid interpretations. Let us suppose, however, that after reading Smith's story you decide that the final paragraph is about the emptiness or shallowness of characters in a romance novel. The implied criticism, then, might be that such novels flatten human experience.

Now you need to apply this criticism to any romance novel you choose. In other words, you are ready to take inventory for subject and purpose. As you begin to play with the three questions, remember that you do not have to follow any order and that you can move freely back and forth from one question to another. For instance, in the sample

---

1. Linda Flower, *Problem-Solving Strategies for Writing*, 3rd Edition (San Diego: Harcourt Brace Jovanovich, 1989).

inventory that follows, the responses to the first and third questions were triggered by beginning with question 2, and by a strong feeling that Smith's criticism of popular romance was justified. Here is what an inventory might look like at the end of the questioning process:

1. What do I know about the subject?

Romance is an illusion—attractive, wealthy people leading exciting lives.

Lots of glamour—what do I mean by this exactly?

Happy endings, happily ever after like fairy tales.

Huge markets.

Written to formula—characters and plots interchangeable.

Smith's story mentions sending away for guidelines. Can I do this? Is there time? What *is* the formula?

Love conquers all, falling in love is exciting.

That moment of falling in love is frozen in time.

2. What is my attitude toward the subject?

Strongly agree with Smith—romance novels are not about real human lives, but about illusory lives.

Why is the illusion so popular?
   Need for escape from everyday problems.
   Desire to believe illusion is true.
   Illusion seemingly supported by movies, popular music,
      even advertisements.

The formula must have mass appeal, universal characters and attractive packaging.

Everyone wants to be in love.

Appeal to human desire, like advertising.

Love for sale.

3. What do I want to convince my reader of?

Too easy just to say romances are silly.

Are romances adult fairy tales?

Maybe part of the satisfaction is recognizing the formula, variations of "once upon a time" and "happily ever after."

The formula is reassuring.

I think I want to suggest that my romance novel—doesn't matter which one I choose because of the formula—is like an advertisement for falling in love.

Appeal to desires and attractive packaging, like good-looking and rich characters, exotic settings, etc.

The advertisement works *because* it seems an easy, attractive solution to serious, complex problems in society such as loneliness and boredom.

Falling in love is a quick fix, readers can relive the moment.

By the end of the questioning process, the inventory generated begins to highlight a link between advertising and romance novels, which is an idea worth pursuing. A different list of what a person knows and feels about the subject would no doubt suggest a different issue to pursue. The advantage of this strategy, in fact, is that it allows you to begin with what you know and then to build on your own information and attitudes to help shape a subject and purpose that are meaningful to you. In this case, the subject is to consider a romance novel as an advertisement for falling in love; the purpose is to support Smith's criticism but also to argue that human experience is deliberately flattened in order to sell more of the product to more people.

At this point, because the assignment has two parts, you might want to rethink or rephrase your initial answer to the framing question so that it fits more closely the direction you want to pursue. Smith's last paragraph, which provides the frame for the assignment, emphasizes the literal meaning of a silhouette: "flat black shapes against the tropic sky." On that basis, you could argue that her implied criticism is that romance novels are all form and attractive appearance at the expense of genuine human problems. This slight rephrasing of Smith's position makes the links between advertising and the novels a bit more obvious and helps pave the way for you to emphasize formula and repetition over minor particularities in your discussion of the romance you choose. Remember that this kind of revision is part of the recursive nature of the composing process, and you will probably return to both the subject and the purpose as you begin to gather more information and draft your ideas.

Planning What and How

This freewriting strategy can help you discover what you want to say and how you can best persuade your reader to accept your point of view. The key to effective freewriting is to allow ideas to flow without worrying about sentence structure or the mechanics of writing, such as spelling or punctuation. Freewriting is pure exploration, writing you do for yourself to help organize and focus your thinking. When you are finished using the strategy, you can keep the promising ideas and throw away the prose.

What and how plans are really maps of where you are in the composing process and so can be used more than once in the preparation of an essay. Here, they are being used to help determine a subject and purpose in response to the challenge to choose your own topic in a course on popular fiction. Some of the issues discussed in the course might include writing to a formula, mass marketing, gender roles, and the appeals made to contemporary issues and values.

Illustration

1. The What Plan

I'm fascinated in the course so far by how some authors just seem to be able to put their finger on an issue that the public is really concerned about. Last week we even talked about how romance novels have a whole formula that exploits one of these issues or needs over and over again. But I'm pretty sick of romances, and lots of other students will probably write about them anyway. So what else is really popular and uses a formula? Stephen King? Yes, but the novels are so long. Maybe something from the past would be easier to find information on. Agatha Christie is still really popular, and so is Sherlock Holmes—I really like those stories and there is a kind of pattern in how they're set up—there's a mystery or crime, Sherlock's powers of observation, clues, Watson getting it wrong, then the surprise solution. I'd like to talk about two or three of those stories in terms of their formula or repeated elements and try to figure out why they're still so popular. Maybe it's the idea of crime? No, it's probably Sherlock himself—how smart he is, how he always wins out in the end.

At the end of the what plan—which ends whenever you run out of ideas or feel that something interesting has popped up—pause for a few minutes and reread what you have. Then think about how you can convince a reader that the Sherlock Holmes stories are a good topic for your course—that what you want to say is important and relevant to course issues. Now you are ready for the second part of the freewriting exercise.

2. *The How Plan*

First I have to pick two or three stories and nail down the formula—the reader has to have enough details to see that the pattern really exists and to know what the pattern is. Then I have to
make an argument that the formula fulfills some desire or some
need that society—then and now—feels. This might be tricky. I
need to find out something about when these stories were written but I don't want to get sidetracked on a historical time frame.
Sherlock is still around so chances are I'm looking for a fairly universal need. Maybe the triumph of good over evil, but I'll need to
make that more specific. Okay—how does this fit the course? The
formula is the key. Maybe I can apply some of the stuff we
learned about romances to the Sherlock stories—the criminal
world as exotic setting? Oh, and we're talking about popular fiction with a mass market so I'll have to give some proof about how
widely read these stories were. Maybe I can use the fact that
Conan Doyle had to bring back Sherlock after killing him off. The
first step is to choose the stories I want to use, and then take a
look at what some critics might say about the formula and its
popularity. If I could write a kind of mock story like Lee Smith
did for romances—only shorter—that might really appeal to my
reader and help make the point about the formula.

Neither of these plans represents the last thoughts that you will have
on subject and purpose, but they provide an initial direction. One of
the reasons for narrowing a subject and trying to articulate a purpose
early in the composing process is to make the gathering of information
more efficient. Here, you will need to analyze no more than three stories in terms of their formula or repeated elements, so you can safely
leave for another time and another essay topic any critical material on
the prose style of Sir Arthur Conan Doyle, his life, or his use of color
symbolism.

These strategies also encourage the writer to begin thinking about
the importance of anticipating the reader's needs. In an academic setting, there is no avoiding the fact that the primary reader will be your
instructor—but you can invent a less intimidating reader for the purposes of composing. Many students find it beneficial to write to a kind
of generic reader who is both intelligent and curious. Your task is to
"teach" that reader about your subject, to anticipate and answer that
reader's questions, and to persuade that reader that what you are saying is relevant to the larger issues in the course you are studying
together.

GENERATING IDEAS

Anyone who has ever written has felt the terror of the blank page—the conviction that there is nothing left to say about a particular subject and that your own ideas, especially, are not worth expressing. There are two obstacles at work here, both of which can seriously interfere with the composing process. The first is a lack of confidence in creativity, and the second, an insistent critical voice, prejudging and dismissing any tentative approaches to creative thinking you might be willing to make. The solution is to learn some specific strategies for generating ideas—strategies that can help you develop your creativity and turn off your mind's critical monitor until you are ready to use it.

The process of generating ideas is active and deliberate. Ideas do not begin to flow just because you want or need them. Thus it is important to engage in specific activities which can help stimulate creative thinking. You need to create a sort of playground for exploration, risk taking, and spontaneity. Inside the playground, there is no monitor or supervisor. In other words, when you are generating ideas—coaxing links and associations and insights onto a page—you are playing with possibilities, not judging them.

The generation of ideas is associated with lateral thinking, that is, with challenging accepted patterns of thought and exploring the least likely pathways to a solution. Lateral thinking is often provocative and linked to humor and speculation. Unlike vertical thinking, which is sequential and logical, lateral thinking is free to explore whatever direction the mind suggests, and no idea is too silly or trivial to pursue. Thus, the three strategies for generating ideas that are discussed—branching, the observer's questions, and the dictionary game—are designed to rescue you from the blank page. Fill up that page with whatever comes into your head, without stopping to organize or judge. When you have finished playing and exploring, you can return to the logical pathways of vertical thinking to develop the two or three ideas that most interest you. The point is to allow yourself to be creative and let the unexpected emerge by being willing to enter the unsupervised playground of lateral thinking.

Branching

Branching is a wonderfully versatile thinking strategy that can be used for many purposes, including gathering and organizing material.

Here, you can use branching as a variation on brainstorming to help generate ideas for an essay on political writing, based on Isabel Allende's published lecture "Writing As an Act of Hope."

As you may already know, to brainstorm, you begin with a key concept or topic, say political writing, and then jot down all the words and ideas you can think of associated with political writing. This is an effective strategy for generating ideas, especially when you are starting from scratch. However, many assignments at the college level do not start from scratch. Instead, you are expected to incorporate the theories and ideas of an expert or experts into your own thinking. For example, you must write an essay on some aspect of political writing, based on what you have learned from reading Allende's piece. It is this added step of incorporating the views of an expert that makes branching such a useful tool. It allows you to map the main points of Allende's speech and at the same time generate ideas about political writing.

Illustration

WRITING AS AN ACT OF HOPE

Isabel Allende

In every interview during the last few years I encountered two questions that forced me to define myself as a writer and as a human being: Why do I write? And who do I write for? Tonight I will try to answer those questions.

In 1981, in Caracas, I put a sheet of paper in my typewriter and wrote the first sentence of *The House of the Spirits:* "Barabbas came to us by sea." At that moment I didn't know why I was doing it, or for whom. In fact, I assumed that no one would ever read it except my mother, who reads everything I write. I was not even conscious that I was writing a novel. I thought I was writing a letter—a spiritual letter to my grandfather, a formidable old patriarch, whom I loved dearly. He had reached almost one hundred years of age and decided that he was too tired to go on living, so he sat in his armchair and refused to drink or eat, calling for Death, who was kind enough to take him very soon.

I wanted to bid him farewell, but I couldn't go back to Chile, and I knew that calling him on the telephone was useless, so I began this letter. I wanted to tell him that he could go in peace because all his memories were with me. I had forgotten nothing. I had all his anecdotes, all the characters of the family, and to prove it I began writing the story of Rose, the fiancée my grandfather had had, who is called Rose the Beautiful in the book. She really existed; she's not a copy from García Márquez, as some people have said.

For a year I wrote every night with no hesitation or plan. Words came out like a violent torrent. I had thousands of untold words stuck in my chest, threatening to choke me. The long silence of exile was turning me to stone; I needed to open a valve and let the river of secret words find a way out. At the end of that year there were five hundred pages on my table; it didn't look like a letter anymore. On the other hand, my grandfather had died long before, so the spiritual message had already reached him. So I thought, "Well, maybe in this way I can tell some other people about him, and about my country, and about my family and myself." So I just organized it a little bit, tied the manuscript with a pink ribbon for luck, and took it to some publishers.

The spirit of my grandmother was protecting the book from the very beginning, so it was refused everywhere in Venezuela. Nobody wanted it—it was too long; I was a woman; nobody knew me. So I sent it by mail to Spain, and the book was published there. It had reviews, and it was translated and distributed in other countries.

In the process of writing the anecdotes of the past, and recalling the emotions and pains of my fate, and telling part of the history of my country, I found that life became more comprehensible and the world more tolerable. I felt that my roots had been recovered and that during that patient exercise of daily writing I had also recovered my own soul. I felt at that time that writing was unavoidable—that I couldn't keep away from it. Writing is such a pleasure; it is always a private orgy, creating and recreating the world according to my own laws, fulfilling in those pages all my dreams and exorcising some of my demons.

But that is a rather simple explanation. There are other reasons for writing.

Six years and three books have passed since *The House of the Spirits.* Many things have changed for me in that time. I can no longer pretend to be naïve, or elude questions, or find refuge in irony. Now I am constantly confronted by my readers, and they can be very tough. It's not enough to write in a state of trance, overwhelmed by the desire to tell a story. One has to be responsible for each word, each idea. Be very careful: the written word cannot be erased.

I began to receive academic papers from American universities about the symbols in my books, or the metaphors, or the colors, or the names. I'm always very scared by them. I just received three different papers on Barabbas, the dog. One of them says that he symbolizes the innocence of Clara because he accompanies her during her youth, and when she falls in love, symbolically, the dog dies in a pool of blood. That means the sexual act, it seems. The second paper says that the dog represents repression—the militarists—and the third paper says that he is the male part of Clara, the hidden, dark, big beast in her. Well, really, Barabbas was just the dog I had at home. And he was killed as it was told in the book. But of course it sounds much better to answer that Barabbas symbolizes the innocence of Clara, so that's the explanation I give when somebody asks.

Maybe the most important reason for writing is to prevent the erosion of time, so that memories will not be blown away by the wind. Write to register history, and name each thing. Write what should not be forgotten. But then, why write novels? Probably because I come from Latin America, a land of crazy, illuminated people, of geological and political cataclysms—a land so large and profound, so beautiful and frightening, that only novels can describe its fascinating complexity.

A novel is like a window, open to an infinite landscape. In a novel we can put all the interrogations, we can register the most extravagant, evil, obscene, incredible or magnificent facts—which, in Latin America, are not hyperbole, because that is the dimension of our reality. In a novel we can give an illusory order to chaos. We can find the key to the labyrinth of history. We can make excursions into the past, to try to understand the present and dream of the future. In a novel we can use everything: testimony, chronicle, essay, fantasy, legend, poetry and other devices that might help us to decode the mysteries of our world and discover our true identity.

For a writer who nourishes himself or herself on images and passions, to be born in a fabulous continent is a privilege. In Latin America we don't have to stretch our imaginations. Critics in Europe and the United States often stare in disbelief at Latin American books, asking how the authors dare to invent those incredible lies of young women who fly to heaven wrapped in linen sheets; of black emperors who build fortresses with cement and the blood of emasculated bulls; of outlaws who die of hunger in the Amazon with bags full of emeralds on their backs; of ancient tyrants who order their mothers to be flogged naked in front of the troops and modern tyrants who order children to be tortured in front of their parents; of hurricanes and earthquakes that turn the world upside down; of revolutions made with machetes, bullets, poems and kisses; of hallucinating landscapes where reason is lost.

It is very hard to explain to critics that these things are not a product of our pathological imaginations. They are written in our history; we can find them every day in our newspapers. We hear them in the street; we suffer them frequently in our own lives. It is impossible to speak of Latin America without mentioning violence. We inhabit a land of terrible contrasts and we have to survive in times of great violence.

Contrast and violence, two excellent ingredients for literature, although for us, citizens of that reality, life is always suspended from a very fragile thread.

The first, the most naked and visible form of violence is the extreme poverty of the majority, in contrast with the extreme wealth of the very few. In my continent two opposite realities coexist. One is a legal face, more or less comprehensible and with a certain pretension to dignity and civilization. The other is a dark and tragic face, which we do not like to show but which is always threatening us. There is an apparent world and a real world—nice neighborhoods where blond children play on their bicycles and servants walk elegant dogs, and other neighborhoods, of slums and garbage, where dark children play naked with hungry mutts. There are offices of marble and steel where young executives discuss the stock market, and forgotten villages where people still live and die as they did in the Middle Ages. There is a world of fiction created by the official discourse, and another world of blood and pain and love, where we have struggled for centuries.

In Latin America we all survive on the borderline of those two realities. Our fragile democracies exist as long as they don't interfere with imperialist interests. Most of our republics are dependent on submissiveness. Our institutions and laws are inefficient. Our armed forces often act as mercenaries for a privileged social group that pays tribute to transnational enterprises. We are living in the worst economic, political and social crisis since the conquest of America by the Spaniards. There are hardly two or three leaders in the whole continent. Social inequality is greater every day, and to avoid an outburst of public rancor, repression also rises day by day. Crime, drugs, misery and ignorance are present in every Latin American country, and the military is an immediate threat to society and civil governments. We try to keep straight faces while our feet are stuck in a swamp of violence, exploitation, corruption, the terror of the state and the terrorism of those who take arms against the status quo.

But Latin America is also a land of hope and friendship and love. Writers navigate in these agitated waters. They don't live in ivory towers; they cannot remove themselves from this brutal reality. In such circumstances there is no time and no wish for narcissistic literature. Very few of our writers contemplate their navel in self-centered monologue. The majority want desperately to communicate.

I feel that writing is an act of hope, a sort of communion with our fellow men. The writer of good will carries a lamp to illuminate the dark corners. Only that, nothing more—a tiny beam of light to show some hidden aspect of reality, to help decipher and understand it and thus to initiate, if possible, a change in the conscience of some readers. This kind of writer is not seduced by the mermaid's voice of celebrity or tempted by exclusive literary circles. He has both feet planted firmly on the ground and walks hand in hand with the people in the streets. He knows that the lamp is very small and the shadows are immense. This makes him humble.

But just as we should not believe that literature gives us any sort of power, neither should we be paralyzed by false modesty. We should continue to write in spite of the bruises and the vast silence that frequently surrounds us. A book is not an end in itself; it is only a way to touch someone—a bridge extended across a space of loneliness and obscurity—and sometimes it is a way of winning other people to our causes.

I believe in certain principles and values: love, generosity, justice. I know that sounds old-fashioned. However, I believe in those values so firmly that I'm willing to provoke some scornful smiles. I'm sure we have the capacity to build a more gentle world—that doing so is our only alternative, because our present equilibrium is very fragile. In literature, we have been told, optimism is dangerous; it flirts with simplicity and is an insurrection against the sacred laws of reason and good taste. But I don't belong to that group of desperate intellectuals. Despair is a paralyzing feeling. It only benefits our enemies.

My second novel, *Of Love and Shadows*, tells about the *desaparecidos*, "the disappeared ones." It's based on a political massacre that took place in Chile in 1973 during the military coup that put an end to 150 years of democracy. The novel denounces repression and the impunity of the murderers, and it had a warm reception from most readers and critics. But it also drew some strong attacks. Some said it was too political and sentimental and not very objective, as if one could be objective about the crimes of a dictatorship. Maybe these critics would have forgiven me, as other writers have been forgiven, if the book had only been a story of horror and bitterness. They didn't like the fact that in the novel solidarity and hope prevail over death and torture. If the main characters, Irene and Francisco, had died in a torture chamber, or at least if the violent experiences they endured had drowned them in despair and destroyed forever their capacity to love and to dream, these critics might have been more tolerant. Evidently it's hard to accept in literature that love can be stronger than hatred, although it frequently is in life.

If my books are going to be classified as political, I hope readers will find out that they are not political for ideological reasons only, but for other, more subtle considerations. They are political precisely because Alba Trueba, in *The House of the Spirits*, who has been raped, tortured and mutilated, is able to reconcile herself with life; because Irene and Francisco, in *Of Love and Shadows*, make love in spite of terror; because in my third novel, *Eva Luna*, Eva defeats the odds of her fate with generosity and candor; because these characters search for truth and have the courage to risk their lives.

I suppose I have the secret ambition to become a great writer, to be able to create stories that will resist the passage of time and the judgment of history. Yes, I know, it's terribly pretentious! But I'm more interested in touching my readers—as many of them as possible—on a spiritual and emotional level. To do this from a feminine point of view is a beautiful challenge in the society I live in. The political literature that some women writers have begun to create is so revolutionary that no wonder many critics are scared. Women are questioning the set of values that have sustained human society since the first apes stood on their feet and raised their eyes to the sky. After centuries of silence, women are taking by assault the exclusive male club of literature. Some women have done it before, of course, struggling against formidable obstacles. But now half of the novels published in Europe and the United States are written by women. Our sisters are using the cutting edge of words to change rules we have always had to obey. Until now, humankind has organized itself according to certain principles that are considered part of nature: we are all born (it has been said) with some original sin; we are basically evil, and without the strict control of religion and laws we would devour each other like cannibals; authority, repression and punishment are necessary to keep us in line. According to these theories, the best proof of our perverse nature is that the world is what it is—a round rock lost in the cosmic nightmare, where abuse, war, inequality and hatred prevail.

But a small group of women and young men are now making the most astonishing statements. Fortunately, most of them work in the best universities, so even if they are only a few, their voices have great impact. These people are questioning everything, starting with our own image as human beings. Until now, men have decided the destiny of this suffering planet, imposing ambition, power and individualism as virtues. (They don't admit this, of course; it is more eloquent to speak of peace and cooperation.) These values are also present in literature. Critics, most of them men, as you probably can guess, have determined what is good in literature—what is valuable or artistic, according to our aesthetic, intellectual and moral patterns—leaving aside the feminine half of the human race, whose opinions on this or any other matter don't interest them.

I think it's time to revise this situation. But it is not the Old Guard who will do it. It will be done by women and by young men who have nothing to lose and therefore have no fear.

In the process of analyzing books, critics have exalted all kinds of literary experiments, some of them quite unbearable. How many books have you tried to read lately and haven't gotten past page fifteen because they were simply boring? Flamboyant literary techniques win awards even though the subject is deplorable. The worst vices are gloried if the writing is elegant. Lies, bitterness and arrogance are forgiven if the language is original and the author already has his laurels. Pessimism is in fashion.

But many novels that don't fit that pattern are now being written by women and by some brave men, not all of them young—for example, García Márquez, who wrote that incredible and sentimental book *Love in the Time of Cholera,* which is a sort of magnificent soap opera about two old people who fall in love, and they love each other for eighty years. It's wonderful.

Those writers are shaking the literary world nowadays because they propose a completely new set of values. They don't accept the old rules anymore. They are willing to examine everything—to invent all over again and to express other ethical and aesthetic values; not always to replace the prevailing ones, but to complement them. It's not a question of changing male chauvinism for militant feminism, but of giving both women and men a chance to become better people and to share the heavy burden of this planet. I believe that this is the true political literature of our time.

All political systems, even revolutions, have been created and directed by men, always within the patriarchal regime. Important philosphical movements have tried to change man and society, but without touching the basis of human relations—that is, inequality of the sexes. Men writers of all periods have written political literature, from *Utopia* to parody, but feminine values have been scorned and women have been denied a voice to express them.

Now, finally, women are breaking the rule of silence and raising a strong voice to question the world. This is a cataclysm. It is a new literature that dares to be optimisitic—to speak of love in opposition to pornography, of compassion against cruelty. It is a literature that's not afraid of colloquial language, of being sentimental if necessary; a literature that searches the spiritual dimension of reality, that accepts the unknown and the unexplainable, confusion and terror; a literature that has no answers, only questions; a literature that doesn't invent history or try to explain the world solely with reason, but also seeks knowledge through feelings and imagination. Maybe, this literature says, it's not true that we are perverse and evil. Maybe the idea of original sin is just a terrible mistake. Maybe we are not here to be punished, because the gods love us and are willing to give us a chance to decipher the clues and trace new paths.

The effect of these books is hard to measure, because the old instruments are no longer useful. Probably the strongest literature being written nowadays is by those who stand unsheltered by the system: blacks, Indians, homosexuals, exiles and, especially, women—the crazy people of the world, who dare to believe in their own force. We dare to think that humanity is not going to destroy itself, that we have the capacity to reach an agreement, not only for survival but also to achieve happiness. That is why we write—as an act of human solidarity and commitment to the future. We want to change the rules, even if we won't live long enough to see the results. We have to make real revolutions of the spirit, of values, of life. And to do so we have to begin dreaming them.

So I will continue to write: about two lovers embracing in the moonlight, near an abandoned mine where they have found the bodies of fifteen peasants, murdered by the military. Or about raped women and tortured men and families who sell themselves as slaves because they are starving. And also—why not?—about golden sunsets and loving mothers and poets who die of love. I want to tell stories and say, for example, that I care more for the free man than the free enterprise, more for solidarity than charity. I want to say that it's more important for me to share than to compete. And I want to write about the necessary changes in Latin America that will enable us to rise from our knees after five centuries of humiliations.

Much skill will be needed to write about these things eloquently. But with patience and hard work I hope to acquire that skill. I suppose I'm being very ambitious. Well, most writers are, even women writers.

Now, for whom do I write?

When I face a clean sheet of paper, I don't think of a large audience or of the people who would raise their knives to cut me in pieces. If I did, terror would paralyze me. Instead, when I write, a benevolent image comes to my mind—that of Alexandra Jorquera, a young woman who lives in Chile whom I scarcely know. She has read my books so many times that she can repeat paragraphs by heart. In fact, she knows them better than I do. She quotes me and I don't know she's quoting me. Once she told me that she had discovered in my books the history of Chile that is denied by the official textbooks of the dictatorship—the forbidden and secret history that nevertheless is still alive in the memories of most Chileans.

This is the best compliment my work has ever received. For the sake of this girl I am very demanding with my writing. Sometimes, tempted by the beauty of a sentence, I am about to betray the truth, and then Alexandra comes to my mind and I remember that she, and others like her, don't deserve that. At other times I'm too explicit, too near the pamphlet. But then I step back, thinking she doesn't deserve that either—to be underestimated. And when I feel helpless against brutality and suffering, her candid face brings back my strength. All writers should have a reader like her, waiting for their words. They would never feel lonely, and their work would have a new and shining dimension.

In Latin America today, 50 percent of the population is illiterate. Among those who can read and write, only very few can buy books, and among those who can buy books, very few have the habit of reading. What, then, is the importance of a book in Latin America? None, would be the reasonable answer. But it's not exactly that way. For some strange reason, the written word has a tremendous impact in that illiterate continent. The totalitarian regimes have persecuted, tortured, sent into exile and murdered many writers. This is not an accident; dictators don't make mistakes in these details. They know that a book can be dangerous for them. In our countries most of the press is controlled by private enterprises or by inefficient governments. Eduardo Galeano, the great writer from Uruguay, puts it bluntly: "Almost all mass media promote a colonialistic culture, which justifies the unjust organization of the world as a result of the legitimate victory of the best—that is, the strongest. They lie about the past and about reality. They propose a lifestyle which postulates consumerism as an alternative to communism, which exalts crime as achievement, lack of scruples as virtue, and selfishness as a natural requirement."

What can writers do against this persistent and powerful message? The first thing we should try to do is write clearly. Not simply—that only works with soap advertising; we don't have to sacrifice aesthetics for the sake of ethics. On the contrary, only if we are able to say it beautifully can we be convincing. Most readers are perfectly able to appreciate subtleties and poetic twists and symbols and metaphors. We should not write with a paternalistic attitude, as if readers were simple-minded, but we should also be aware of elaborate and unnecessary ornamentation, which frequently hides a lack of ideas. It has been said that we Spanish-speaking people have the vice of empty words, that we need six hundred pages to say what would be better told in fifty.

The opportunity to reach a large number of readers is a great responsibility. Unfortunately, it is hard for a book to stand against the message of the mass media; it's an unfair battle. Writers should therefore look for other forms of expressing their thoughts, avoiding the prejudice that only in books can they make literature. All means are legitimate, not only the cultivated language of academia but also the direct language of journalism, the mass language of radio, television and the movies, the poetic language of popular songs and the passionate language of talking face to face with an audience. These are all forms of literature. Let us be clever and use every opportunity to introduce ourselves in the mass media and try to change them from within.

In Venezuela, José Ignacio Cabrujas, a playwright and novelist, one of the most brilliant intellectuals of the country, writes soap operas. These shows are the most important cultural phenomenon in Latin America. Some people watch three or four a day, so you can imagine how important that kind of writing is. Cabrujas doesn't elude reality. His soap operas show a world of contrasts. He presents problems such as abortion, divorce, machismo, poverty and crime. The result is quite different from "Dynasty." But it's also very successful.

I tried to put some of that soap opera stuff in *Eva Luna,* because I'm fascinated by that version of reality. The ladies on TV wear false eyelashes at eleven in the morning. The difference between rich and poor is that the rich wear cocktail gowns all the time and the poor have their faces painted black. They all go blind or become invalids and then they recover. Just like real life!

Many of the most important Latin American writers have been journalists, and they go back to it frequently because they are aware that their words in a newspaper or on the radio reach an audience that their books can never touch. Others write for the theater or the movies, or write lyrics for popular songs. All means are valid if we want to communicate and don't presume to be writing only for an educated elite or for literary prizes.

In Latin America a book is almost a luxury. My hairdresser calls me Dr. Allende because I usually carry a book, and she probably thinks that a doctorate is the minimum prerequisite for such an extravagance. In Chile a novel of three hundred pages can cost the equivalent of a laborer's monthly wages. In some other countries—like Haiti, for example—85 percent of the population is illiterate. Elsewhere in Latin America, nothing is published in the Indian languages of the majority. Many publishers have been ruined by the economic crisis, and the price of books imported from Spain is very high.

However, we should not despair. There is some hope for the spirit. Literature has survived even in the worst conditions. Political prisoners have written stories on cigarette paper. In the wars of Central America, little soldiers, fourteen years old, write poetry in their school notebooks. The Pieroa Indians, those who haven't yet been exterminated by the genocide being carried out against the aborigines of the Amazon, have published some legends in their language.

In my continent, writers often have more prestige than they do in any other part of the world. Some writers are considered witch doctors, or prophets, as if they were illuminated by some sort of natural wisdom. Jorge Amado has to spend part of the year away from Brazil in order to write, because people crowd into his house seeking advice. Mario Vargas-Llosa directs the opposition to Alan Garcia's government in Peru. García Márquez is a frequent middleman for Central American presidents. In Venezuela, Arturo Uslar Pietri is consulted on issues like corruption and oil. These writers have interpreted their reality and told it to the world. Some of them even have the gift of foretelling the future and put in words the hidden thoughts of their people, which of course include social and political problems, because it is impossible to write in a crystal bubble, disregarding the conditions of their continent.

No wonder Latin American novels are so often accused of being political.

For whom do I write, finally? Certainly for myself. But mainly for others, even if there are only a few. For those who have no voice and for those who are kept in silence. For my children and my future grandchildren. For Alexandra Jorquera and others like her. I write for you.

And why do I write? García Márquez once said that he writes so that his friends will love him more. I think I write so that people will love each other more. Working with words is a beautiful craft, and in my continent, where we still have to name all things one by one, it has a rich and profound meaning.

First read Allende's speech. Then take a fresh sheet of paper and write down her title in the center of the page. You are going to branch out from that center, with each branch representing a different pathway you might explore. Actually drawing the branches radiating from the central idea will help free you from linear patterns of thinking. You may also want to time this exercise to ensure that branching continues for at least ten minutes without the interference of premature judging or evaluation of ideas. If you are blocked at any point, simply begin a new branch, turning the paper around as you go along. Again, this action of drawing and turning sometimes allows an evasive idea to emerge. Remember that no idea is too silly or too absurd to include.

Here is one example of a completed branching exercise:

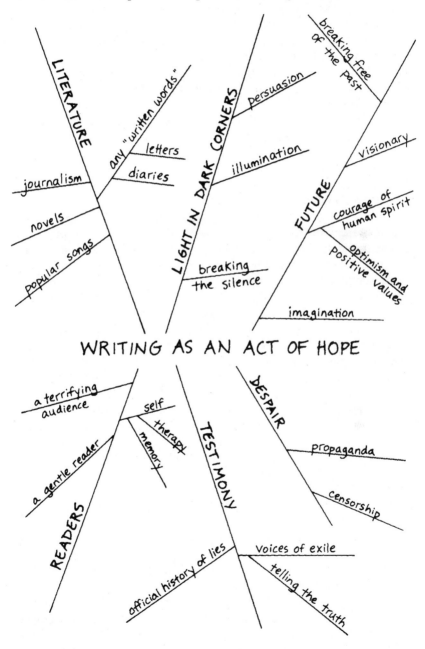

WRITING AS AN ACT OF HOPE

LITERATURE
any "written words"
journalism
letters
diaries
novels
popular songs

LIGHT IN DARK CORNERS
persuasion
illumination
breaking the silence

FUTURE
breaking free of the past
visionary
courage of human spirit
optimism and positive values
imagination

READERS
a terrifying audience
a gentle reader
self
therapy
memory

TESTIMONY
official history of lies
voices of exile
telling the truth

DESPAIR
propaganda
censorship

Even though your own reading of Allende's essay may have emphasized different ideas, notice how many pathways have emerged that can now be explored more fully in an essay on political writing. Branching is really a form of branching out—into new territory, new ideas, and fresh approaches. Initially, it may seem that there is little to say about political writing that has not already been said, and said more eloquently by Allende than it would be possible for you to say. Branching, however, helps illuminate other possibilities to explore. You could investigate the political content of popular music, develop the idea of writers as exiles, or consider history and diaries as forms of political writing. Branching may enable you to appreciate Allende's words as a starting point rather than as the last that might be said on the subject.

Observer's Questions

The strategy of the observer's questions is based on a strategy for generating ideas developed by tagmemicists, people who study the fundamental structures of language. From physics, which studies the fundamental structures of matter, the tagmemicists borrowed the concept of viewing phenomena from three different perspectives: as a particle, as a wave, and as a field. Each observer's question is based on one of these perspectives.

When you are considering your essay topic as a particle, the observer's question would be "What is the nature of the thing itself?" To answer it, you need to view your topic as an object that can be described in detail and is made up of specific parts. The next question, "How has the thing changed?" invites you to consider your subject as a wave, or as an action or process, that changes over time. Finally, to see your topic as part of a field, you need to view it as part of a larger system or network. Here, the observer's question would be "How does the thing fit into a larger category?"

Let us suppose that you have been asked to write an essay that relates Yusef Komunyakaa's poem "Facing It" to "Writing As an Act of Hope" by Isabel Allende. You can use the observer's questions to look at your subject as a particle, as a wave, and as a field.

Illustration

As a Particle: "What is the nature of the thing itself?"
I have two things to consider—the poem and the published speech. The poem is written in memory of those

who died in the Vietnam War. It describes the War Memorial and people visiting it—lots of reference to names carved in stone, and use of light and dark imagery. Komunyakaa was also a journalist who spent time in Vietnam.

The speech is about Allende's own writing, especially her first novel. She talks about the need to preserve her own memories, but also those of her people who have been silenced or exiled. Lots of emphasis on "testimony," on preserving the truth. When she talks about "writing as an act of hope," she refers specifically to a lamp illuminating "the dark corners."

As a Wave: "How has the thing changed?"
In what ways are the poem and the speech actions? What about changing over time? Both might be described as an active or creative way of preserving the memories of the dead, or of reminding us of the human costs of war and oppression. Allende leaves no doubt that writing is a political act, a way of challenging official history. Is the poem a part of history that is seldom written? Is writing a way of reclaiming the past in order to create a different future? The poem seems much more an act of mourning than Allende's speech about hope—maybe mourning is part of a process of healing, the first step toward hope.

As a Field: "How does the thing fit into a larger category?"
Now I'm looking for a larger context—a way of seeing my two subjects as part of a larger network. Well, the poem fits in easily with all kinds of TV shows, movies, and novels about Vietnam. Most try to cope with the pain and loss of innocence, but some (Rambo!) glorify war.

Allende is a Latin American—she talks about this context as one filled with incredible events and contrasts. Maybe war is like that—an incredible reality filled with extremes, exotic settings. In a way, the speech is the context for the poem. I mean the poem can be seen as one example of the kind of writing Allende is describing—except for the optimism. I can't see the poem as very hopeful. Remembering the ghosts of the dead is important to Allende, but in the poem the ghosts still seem to be suffering.

The observer's questions can help you open up a topic, and view it from different perspectives. This strategy is especially useful when you are convinced that there is only one way to look at a certain set of ideas or only one way to relate one idea to another. With the ideas generated here, for instance, you might choose to develop one of several possible relationships: the poem as an example of political writing as testimony or as a challenge to official history or as an act of mourning and healing or as an exception to Allende's sense of hope.

The Dictionary Game

Of all the strategies for generating ideas, the dictionary game, invented by Edward de Bono and originally described as random word stimulation, can be the most fun.[2] The object of the game is to choose at random ten nouns from a standard college dictionary, and then to make whatever associations you can between those words and the subject you are considering. As in most lateral thinking exercises, the key to success in applying this particular strategy is to *play* with unexpected or unusual associations. The ten nouns you choose at random will be your triggers, inviting you to think about your subject in fresh and provocative ways.

Illustration

Suppose that you have been asked to write a reader response essay, based on Yusef Komunyakaa's poem "Facing It." In other words, you have to write a short, critical essay that argues for a particular interpretation of the poem and assigns meaning to it based on its textual features. First, after reading the poem, jot down your initial responses. You might write that the poem makes you think about those who died and those who survived the Vietnam War.

FACING IT

Yusef Komunyakaa

My black face fades,
hiding inside the black granite.

2. Edward de Bono, *Lateral Thinking* (London: Penguin Books, 1990) 173–80.

I said I wouldn't,
dammit: No tears.
I'm stone. I'm flesh.
My clouded reflection eyes me
like a bird of prey, the profile of night
slanted against morning. I turn
this way—the stone lets me go.
I turn that way—I'm inside
the Vietnam Veterans Memorial
again, depending on the light
to make a difference.
I go down the 58,022 names,
half-expecting to find
my own in letters like smoke.
I touch the name Andrew Johnson;
I see the booby trap's white flash.
Names shimmer on a woman's blouse
but when she walks away
the names stay on the wall.
Brushstrokes flash, a red bird's
wings cutting across my stare.
The sky. A plane in the sky.
A white vet's image floats
closer to me, then his pale eyes
look through mine. I'm a window.
He's lost his right arm
inside the stone. In the black mirror
a woman's trying to erase names:
no she's brushing a boy's hair.

Now look up any ten nouns from a standard college dictionary. Do not exclude any choices; in fact, open the dictionary at random ten times and write down the first noun you find on a given page. Here is a list of nouns generated by following the random method:

bunch	plunder
discourse	robe
guidepost	sponge
matins	tetrad
palate	wildflower

However strange your list may seem at first, use the dictionary words to explore new ways of approaching the poem. You may start anywhere you like, go through the dictionary list in order, or begin with the associations you feel are most obvious. For example, *plunder* refers to the spoils of war, something taken by force. It usually consists of objects—stolen goods such as food, jewelry, paintings, or household goods. In "Facing It," however, the poet is not concerned with loss of property, but with the loss of friends and even loss of innocence. Seeing these losses as an invisible or emotional kind of plunder gives you an unusual way of writing about the poem.

Similarly, *matins* is a word for morning prayers; you might see the poem as a kind of prayer for peace or healing. *Guideposts* are signs that give us directions or help us find our way. Can you imagine the Vietnam Veterans War Memorial as a kind of emotional or moral guidepost? The word *discourse* from the list may stimulate you to look more closely at the language of the poem. Discourse often means a form of rational argument. What is the poem arguing for, and is it appealing to rationality?

Even words from the list that may seem to have no connection with your subject can yield creative associations. A sponge, for example, absorbs water and is used for cleaning. Think of the poem's speaker as soaking up the images he sees when he visits the memorial or of trying to wipe clean his painful memories. Tetrad means a group or arrangement of four—and there are four people in the poem aside from the speaker. What might these people represent for the poet? In looking for groups of four in the poem, you might also notice that the word *stone* is used three times, and its synonym *granite* is used once. Clearly, "stone" refers to the War Memorial itself, but the word also makes us think of something cold and unyielding—a stony heart or a stone's face.

Keep playing with the trigger words as long as you feel they are helping you to understand the poem and explore it from fresh angles. If you get stuck on a word from your list, skip it and try another. Remember that the correctness of your ideas is not at issue here. Allow yourself to play. At first, *wildflower* may seem to have no connection with the poem at all, but it may make you think of something beautiful and short-lived, or of something blooming unexpectedly in a wild place. Both of these associations are worth exploring in the poem.

When you finish playing the dictionary game, consider all the ideas you have generated. You may well have one or two original insights that you can now develop in your writing, and certainly you will have a deeper understanding of the richness of the poem.

ORGANIZING STRATEGIES

Most people would agree that the way in which material is presented to them is an important factor in how well that material is understood. Imagine that you have just attended two different lectures: in the first, the instructor seemed to drift arbitrarily from topic to topic, throwing out ideas like tiny pearls of wisdom; in the second, the instructor used the blackboard to outline the lecture, thus giving the audience not only ideas, but also information as to how those ideas interrelate. Although there is no question that the second lecture will be better understood by a majority of students, there is still an attraction to scattering pearls. Despite the easily proven necessity for arranging material in such a way as to make it more accessible and more comprehensible, the concept of organization has about it a sense of dullness, of duty work, of plodding along in the composing process.

Why are decisions about how best to present your written material viewed as uncreative? After all, a thoughtful consideration of how to structure other activities in our lives is often both natural and fun. The games people play, from organized sports to ticktacktoe, are structured; the music people listen to is structured, and one of the pleasures associated with listening to jazz is detecting variations in structure. Even telling jokes is a structured art—no matter how funny the content of the joke, the humor is lost unless the teller has a flair for delivering punch lines. Yet the activity of organizing an essay is rarely associated with words such as "flair" and "pleasure." Instead, this part of writing has become overburdened with words like "mechanical" and phrases like "be more logical."

It is perhaps not surprising, then, that one of the most common criticisms of student essays is that they are poorly organized. First, it must be admitted that this criticism is sufficiently vague to cover a range of ills and is sometimes used as a kind of catchall phrase when a more precise reason for a problem in communicating is not easy to determine. Nonetheless, in many instances the criticism is justified, and there may be many reasons why pearls of wisdom have been merely scattered across a page rather than strung into a necklace. Not the least of these reasons is that the organization of essays often modeled for students seems to be restrictive.

Consider the traditional ways in which the overall organization of an essay is often planned out. There are, of course, variations on the traditional plan, but the following would be a typical example:

I. First Major Heading or Main Idea

    A. Division of that

        1. subset

        2. subset

    B. Division of that

II. Second Major Heading or Main Idea

    A. Division of that

        1. subset

        2. subset

    B. Division of that

        1. subset

        2. subset

You can extend this topic outline until all of your major ideas have been included. It works on the principles of division and subordination: first divide your essay into several large chunks or categories and then group the relevant smaller and supporting ideas under the appropriate category. The model appeals to common sense, and it looks really good on the page.

The problem is that the model also looks a little frightening, and for good reason. It is too linear, too sequential; B follows A, but comes before C no matter what. Thought processes are seldom so orderly, and the model does not seem to take into account the recursiveness of the composing process. In fact, the outline cannot be done until near the very end of the process—in time, perhaps, to help the reader but offering very little to the writer in the early stages of drafting and revising. Defenders of these sorts of plans point out that they are not meant to be etched in stone and can be changed at any time. But it is unlikely that a person would be willing to undo too quickly all that hard work of division and subordination.

Yet the question remains, why is this organizing strategy restrictive? To answer the question, you need to apply this kind of model to an essay you are working on and note how it begins to influence your thinking. For example, say you are writing about images of masculinity in popular romance fiction. The outline you draw up might look like this, and, to be fair, the model itself seems less scary when it is filled in with actual ideas:

Images of Masculinity in Popular Romance

I. Males as Attractive Packaging

    A. Physical appearance

        1. Tall, dark, handsome

        2. Strong, active, athletic

    B. Masculine traits

II. Males as Rescuers

    A. Knight in shining armor

        1. Heroic qualities

        2. Protective

    B. Breadwinner

        1. Rich and successful

        2. Higher social status

As noted earlier, you can expand the outline to fit in all your ideas. Indeed, it is this notion of fitting in ideas that makes the model restrictive: some people describe it as fitting round ideas into square holes. If you find your focus shifting from what you want to say to thinking about how the model looks—should heroic qualities be subdivided? is protective really a subset?—then the rigid, linear, and parallel form of the outline is starting to swallow up your content.

The very neatness of this model contributes to its restrictiveness. A subdivision with the potential to become a major heading may remain unexplored or undeveloped once you have categorized it as minor or subordinate. In short, the model lacks fluidity, imposing itself on the ideas that have already been generated and making less likely the generation of new ideas. It is no wonder that organization begins to seem an uncreative chore when it is allowed to curtail the writer's freedom of expression.

Organizing strategies, however, *can* be quick, expansive, and creative. For example, you can use branching several times throughout the composing process—starting early enough in the process to help you refine ideas and generate new ones. Another method, a three-step strategy for organizing ideas, which consists of developing a controlling sentence, using that sentence as a basis for an issue tree, and then freewriting an argumentative plan, also allows you ample opportunity for revision and creativity. Both these approaches stress the importance of content as the starting point. Since the content determines the patterns of organization that might be possible, there is no set pattern of organization into which ideas must be squeezed and manipulated.

Branching

The strategy of branching is described in the previous section as a method for generating ideas. This fact alone should help you see that organizing does not have to mean the abandonment of creative thinking. In fact, early attempts at organizing your material can actually focus and sharpen your creative thinking. Begin your branching exercise at the center of the page, radiating lines outward and returning to the center. This fluid, back-and-forth pattern closely resembles the recursive nature of the composing process itself. There is plenty of room for additions, omissions, and afterthoughts as you explore ways of developing a core, or central, idea.

Illustration

Here is a branching outline for the topic "Images of Masculinity in Popular Romances." The phrase or sentence stating the subject is placed in the center of the page, and each branch radiating from that center explores a different aspect of the subject.

When you actually try branching yourself, you will be able to experience the ways in which it can trigger ideas and help clarify relationships among them. Here, for example, you can see how the notion of formula flows from the center and along all of the branches in an investigation of formulaic or stereotypical roles. The act of drawing in the branches led to the insight that these "fantasy" males are reflections of cultural stereotypes about both masculine traits and behavior *and* feminine needs and desires. In other words, these men are based on a romance novelist's view of what a woman needs, or, more likely, on the publisher's view since it is the publisher who dictates the guidelines. This information—the restriction of possibilities for masculine behavior and the manipulation of female desire—can now be incorporated into the purpose of the essay, which is to expose the transformation of love into a marketable commodity.

Branching is effective because it utilizes both vertical and lateral thinking: it is spontaneous, yet also logical. It provides an overview of the essay material, as well as some key details. Finally, it is both visual and verbal: you can see the subject with all of its branches all at once

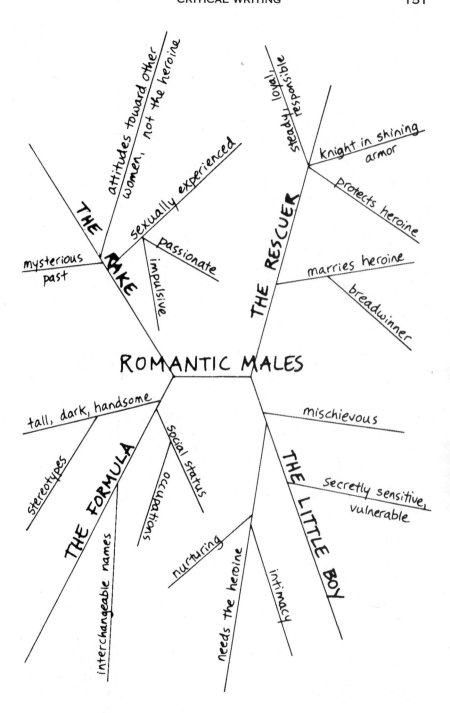

THE RAKE
attitudes toward other women, not the heroine
sexually experienced
passionate
impulsive
mysterious past

THE RESCUER
steady, loyal, responsible
knight in shining armor
protects heroine
marries heroine
breadwinner

ROMANTIC MALES

THE FORMULA
tall, dark, handsome
stereotypes
social status
occupations
interchangeable names

THE LITTLE BOY
mischievous
secretly sensitive, vulnerable
nurturing
needs the heroine
intimacy

and can name those branches by using single words and short phrases that encode larger chunks of information to be recalled later. Best of all, you do not need to worry about fitting ideas into a sequential, linear pattern. Here, the pattern comes from internal logic; it grows out of the ideas themselves.

A Three-Step Strategy for Organizing Ideas

The three-step strategy—a process of thinking through and revising what it is you want to say—resembles the linear development of traditional outlines but allows for more freedom of expression. Just like the larger composing process, this strategy is recursive; however, you begin by trying to phrase a controlling sentence. You then draw an issue tree based on that sentence and finally do a freewriting plan of your argument. Each of these three activities is in itself a method of organizing ideas; used in tandem, they can help you gain control of the composing process.

Step 1: Develop a Controlling Sentence

The controlling sentence of an essay, sometimes called the thesis or thesis statement, contains the central argument and major purpose that you want to communicate. It states, as precisely as possible, the answer or answers that you wish to defend in response to the question or questions implied by the assignment. For example, in the assignment "Discuss the images of masculinity in popular romances," the questions implied are, "What are the images of masculinity in popular romances?" and "Why are they significant?" Your answer to these questions, based on a good deal of thinking and research, becomes the basis of a controlling sentence, which then shapes and directs the remainder of your essay.

Illustration

To be useful to both reader and writer, a controlling sentence must be as specific as possible. Suppose that in response to the assignment just given you wrote the following controlling sentence: "This essay will explore the images of masculinity in popular romances and discuss some of the reasons why they are used." Clearly, this sentence is not very helpful: it merely rephrases the assignment questions without answering them, and so offers neither the reader nor the writer any guidance. The chief distinguishing feature of this kind of controlling sentence is that it can be written immediately, before the writer has done any reading, research, or thinking about specific answers.

Now suppose that after generating and developing some ideas about the subject you wrote the following as a tentative controlling sentence: "As part of the formula of romances, males are confined to stereotyped traits and roles in order to appeal to a mass market of female consumers." This sentence gives the reader some notion of what to expect in the essay—there will be a discussion of formula, some details about stereotyped roles, and some arguments around the concept of consumerism and advertising. The sentence will also help you order evidence and material before beginning a first draft. Often, the writing of the first draft will serve to sharpen your focus even more, allowing for a further rewriting of the controlling sentence in increasingly specific terms: "In his roles as the rescuer, the rake, and the little boy, the hero of the romance formula is carefully packaged to appeal to equally stereotyped female desires and needs."

There are no rules about when is the best time to attempt an initial phrasing of the controlling sentence. Some writers prefer to attempt a statement as soon as they have done some reading and thinking about the topic; others prefer to write an exploratory first draft to help determine what their answers will be. You must follow whatever pattern of composing works best for you. Keep in mind, however, that expert writers accept the necessity of rewriting and rethinking the controlling sentence several times.

Whatever sentence you eventually decide on should appear early in the final draft in order to provide context and organization for the material that follows. The whole point of working so patiently for the exact wording of the controlling sentence is to allow it to control and coordinate your supporting evidence and arguments, which are developed in the body of the essay. For some students, placing the controlling sentence in the introductory paragraph of the final draft can seem awkward and even intimidating. They claim that they would like to keep their reader in suspense rather than give everything away; or they worry that the essay will be doomed from the start if their controlling argument is wrong. If you share either of these views, keep in mind the lecturer who keeps you in suspense about the main point until you are completely muddled, instead of telling you up front what to look for during the lecture. And remember that thinking in terms of right and wrong is often a kind of intellectual straightjacket. There are often many reasonable answers to a question, and what counts is being able to articulate your answers clearly and persuasively. An effective controlling sentence actually protects you because it tells the reader which point of view out of many you have chosen to develop and defend. Instead of trying to cover everything, you need only include and explain material relevant to your controlling argument.

Step 2: Draw an Issue Tree

Like branching, issue trees are an informal and flexible method for organizing the information you have gathered. Drawing an issue tree allows you to construct an overview of your topic so that you can see quickly which parts of your essay are well developed, and which parts require some further thinking. While not nearly so linear or cumbersome as the traditional models of organization, issue trees are based on the principle of a hierarchy: major or more general categories of information appear at the top of the issue tree, with the most specific information at the bottom.

Illustration

Suppose that you have been asked to apply Allende's views of political writing to a text of your own choice. When reading "Writing As an Act of Hope," you are particularly interested in the idea of diaries as examples of political writing, so you begin to narrow your subject by choosing to write about *The Diary of Anne Frank* as an example of political testimony. Once you have generated and gathered enough material to answer the key question, "How is *The Diary of Anne Frank* an example of political testimony?" you are ready to attempt an initial controlling statement, which will act as the base of your issue tree.

Controlling sentence: Written in the midst of oppression, *The Diary of Anne Frank* is a testimony to truth and hope.

Issue Tree:

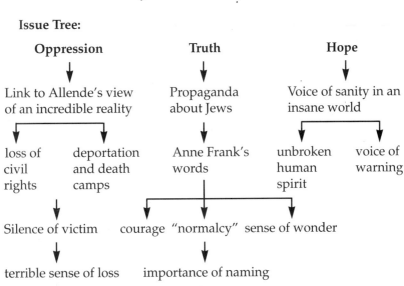

This issue tree charts the core ideas you might have so far about the topic and acts as a kind of visual pointer to ideas that need amplifying or rethinking. You can see that there is not much information to place under the heading "Hope"; therefore, you have to make some creative decisions about whether to keep or omit that category of information. Suppose that you decide to incorporate these ideas under the heading "Anne Frank's words." Suppose, too, that the act of drawing the issue tree has triggered some new ideas, and you now want to examine more closely the notion of silence. After rewording the controlling sentence to allow for the new direction in thinking, you can easily sketch a revised issue tree:

Revised controlling statement: *The Diary of Anne Frank* uses both words and silence as political testimony; her words name a personal truth in the midst of lies, while her eventual silence warns us of the need to take action against oppression.

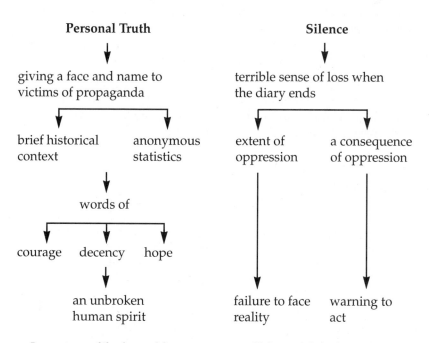

Issue trees, like branching, grow out of ideas rather than impose a structure on ideas. Consequently, they can be easily changed to suit your needs and interests. When you are satisfied that your outline adequately plots the core information you have so far, you can move on to the third step of the organizing strategy.

Step 3: Freewriting an Argumentative Plan

In most cases, the key words you choose for the issue tree identify both information and ideas about it that will help you begin to formulate or reconstruct an argument. Before beginning a full draft, however, some students like to complement the controlling statement and issue tree with a freewriting exercise that spells out their approach and attitudes in more detail. As in other freewriting exercises, remember that this is writing you do for yourself to help you discover and clarify your goals; therefore, you need not worry about style and grammar. Direct your attention to what you want to argue and what your reader will need to know in order to be persuaded.

Illustration

Here is an example of how you can begin transforming the information from an issue tree into an argument. Start your plan with the most recent version of your controlling statement so that the full answer you are defending can guide your thinking.

Controlling statement:

The Diary of Anne Frank uses both words and silence as political testimony; her words name a personal truth in the midst of lies, while her eventual silence warns us of the need to take action against oppression.

Set up the argument:

In my introduction, I need to explain what Allende means by political testimony and why a diary is a good choice of material—I might use her quote about written words bringing light to the dark corners. Then maybe link that sense of darkness to the Holocaust and move right into the facts about Anne Frank and her family. I have to be brief here about background—I can fill in more as I go along. The point is to let the reader know that the diary works in two ways as political testimony—both in what it says and in what it doesn't say or can no longer say when Anne is captured.

Talk about Anne's words first:

Here I want to focus on the diary itself, and how the actual words give a face, name, and personality to a victim of oppression.

The diary acts as a counterpoint to the anonymity of statistics and to stereotypes about Jews. I can work in Allende again to keep reminding my reader that this is testimony—the importance of witnessing, remembering, and truth. Also, I'll want to quote bits of the diary that best demonstrate Anne's values. I want to stress her courage, her struggle to lead a normal life, and her dreams. It makes sense to start with Anne's words, because I have to set up the more difficult and less obvious use of silence.

Explain silence as testimony:

This is going to be tricky, and I think I might need a transition paragraph that tells the reader what I mean by this. I want to argue that the ending of the diary, the point when the words end, is a terrible moment. The light goes out. So the silence becomes a powerful warning about oppression. The awful thing is that Anne's words didn't protect her, no matter how much they've helped future generations. So I have to help the reader see that the silence can ironically mean two things—that Anne couldn't grasp or couldn't face the extent of the forces ranged against her and that the ultimate victory of oppression is the silencing of its victims. In the end, it is important to act, and maybe this is what the words we have left from that time are telling us. So now I have to back this up with some accurate historical information and by pointing out "gaps" in the diary.

Conclusion:

I don't want my reader to be totally depressed, so I will need to re-emphasize the positive values discussed earlier. Going back to Allende's sense of hope for the future will also help and can round out the argument by stressing the value of testimony.

By the end of the freewriting exercise—and of the three-step strategy for organization—you should have enough guidelines and confidence to begin writing a first draft. You may even find the actual writing easier, for you have already made some important decisions about content and how to organize it. No doubt your reader will appreciate organizing strategies, but when they are used creatively and flexibly, they are even more helpful to you as a writer.

Revision Strategies

The hair-pulling frustration of the writer searching for just the right name, the right word, or the right phrase is the part of the revision process that most people understand well. Most also believe that to some extent the search is worthwhile because the right word can "save" an essay, or, as Gary Larson implies in his cartoon, it can turn a heap of scrap paper into a classic. Yet a search without a strategy to guide it seems endless—it is quite a stretch from "Call me Larry" to the published first sentence of *Moby Dick*, "Call me Ishmael." If the real writer had had only a "scratch-out-and-start-over" strategy, we might all still be waiting to read the novel. Indeed, Larson's cartoon is effective not just because of the huge gap in tone between Larry and Ishmael, but also because the situation captured is such a familiar one:

how *does* the process of revision work? Is it really a matter of hit or miss? And when should revision take place?

First of all, revision means *re*seeing, *re*thinking, or *re*conceptualizing whatever is being written in order to make it clearer to the writer and more accessible to the reader. As such, revising involves some fairly complex thinking skills and is a vital part of the recursive composing process. You might generate some ideas and then revise the purpose of your essay; or you might write a first draft and use it to help revise your controlling statement, and so on. In other words, revision is a much more sophisticated process than merely changing a word here and there and tidying up spelling and punctuation a few hours before the essay is due.

Besides being an ongoing process, revision involves different kinds of activities and different levels of attention. Early in the composing process, you may find that directing your attention to word choice impedes the flow of your ideas. Such matters are best left to a later cycle of revision, so that you can concentrate on revising subject and purpose or on shaping and reshaping your argument. Most students do not think about the ways in which they refine their ideas, tinker with their controlling statements, or test their arguments by freewriting as part of revising at all, even though these kinds of rethinking and rewriting activities are often the most valuable and productive parts of the revision process. Revision is part of discovering what you want to say and how you want to proceed. It also involves imagining and anticipating the needs of your reader, and this concern guides decisions about your purposes and your planning—decisions that are usually put into effect well before decisions about vocabulary and sentence structure. If you read some of the earlier parts of this section of the handbook, you will be able to see how many of the strategies for generating and organizing ideas also lead naturally to the kinds of rethinking and reconceptualizing activities that are a part of the early cycles of revision.

A persistence in defining revision to mean merely *reviewing* rather than *rewriting* causes many problems. When you write again, you think again, partly because writing and thinking are so closely connected. When you review, you tend to see the text you are reading as more or less finished, and so you are only concerned with tidying it up rather than changing its meaning. In practical terms, reviewing seems to imply, "Now I have finished writing the essay. I'll just check it for mechanics." Predictably, the strategies available to you at this point are pretty limited and are focused at the sentence and word level. Even if you sense that a certain part of the essay is unclear, you are more likely to try to fix it by changing some words and perhaps raiding the the-saurus than to reconceptualize it. Most students stop reviewing when their essay seems to conform to all the rules they know about writing, even when some of those rules are too outdated or rigid, such as "Never use 'I' in an essay" or "Never start a sentence with 'but.'" In fact, during this last reading of the essay, chances are high that you are not reading for meaning at all but in order to avoid the dreaded red pen, which will surely descend whenever a rule is broken.

To be fair, there does come a time and place in the composing process for revision at the word and perhaps even rule level. The prob-lem is that many students do not have strategies for any *other* kind of revision. They may sense that something is wrong, something bigger than can be fixed with a word, but the only remedy they know, short of starting over, is word substitution. Nor is starting over as easy as it sounds. Aside from time constraints, once you have begun thinking about a topic in a certain way or in a certain pattern, it is very difficult to see it with fresh eyes, especially if you have not had much opportu-nity to practice lateral thinking skills. If revision really is reseeing, dis-covering new pathways, and extending meaning, what are your options?

The first strategy recommended here is the one that everyone knows but seldom applies: give yourself enough time during the composing process to let ideas incubate, to let yourself experiment, and to let your-self walk away and do something else for a while. These scheduled breaks in the composing process are the surest way of helping you see what you are writing with fresh eyes, or with the eyes of a reader. At various points during the process of writing an essay, you must be both writer and reader; that is, you must create and shape a piece of writing and also be able to critique it. Many novice writers believe that their ideas can be interpreted in only one way and that the sense of what they have written is clear; then, a few days later, after gaining some dis-tance from their prose, they are able to see the gaps and leaps in logic that might confuse a reader. Most people have experienced this shift in perspective about their own writing, which is made possible simply by the passage of time, yet most people continue to write to deadlines, which make this strategy a luxury rather than a habit.

Fortunately, there are some strategies you can learn that will help you develop the skills of reading your own essay as you would read any other text, that is, without making the assumption that the mean-ing of the text is fixed. Three specific strategies—"talking" to your reader, writing a "meta-note," and creating a personalized revision sheet—can help you use revision as a way of increasing your understanding of your own process of composing and as a way of articulating your goals in communication.

"Talking" to Your Reader

This first strategy is a way of patterning a conversation with yourself, since at various points in the composing process you are both writer and reader. The kind of reader you imagine or pretend to be when you are writing influences how and what you might write. A reader who dominates the conversation—who is relentlessly critical and judgmental—may well drive you into silence. A reader who is too quiet will not be able to give you much guidance.

One of the most effective ways of "talking" to your reader is to anticipate questions that might be asked about your writing. Most reading strategies are questioning strategies, and applying questions to your own writing is a way of helping you "hear" and "see" gaps in communication. In addition, this strategy is particularly useful if one of the recurring criticisms of your writing is that you need to expand or further develop your ideas. "Develop further" is a quick way of saying that the reader has unanswered questions. By trying to raise and answer some of those questions, you will have a revision strategy for adding depth and detail to your writing.

Illustration

Suppose that you have written the following paragraph about the physical characteristics of males in popular romances. The paragraph includes ideas generated by a branching exercise you completed earlier. The purpose you have decided on at this point is to link the "packaging" of men and advertisements:

> The fantasy male of popular romance is pure formula—tall, dark, handsome, and successful. Physical presence is often "imposing," a word used to describe the hero, Marc Adams, in *Ariana's Magic*, a Harlequin Romance written by Judy Kaye. Similarly, Lee Smith describes Rock Cliff as having "a rugged, virile form." The names, as long as they are manly, are interchangeable. Of course, a real man also has to be socially successful—Rock Cliff is a brooding, artistic novelist, and Adams is a wealthy lawyer. No matter what the specific details, the heroine is swept away.

After finishing your first draft and assessing it against your branching outline, you decide that this paragraph is a little thin. In the outline, this part of the plan represented one whole branch, or section, of the argument. Now it is just one fairly short paragraph. The time has come to decide whether the idea is really as crucial to your argument as you first supposed. If you decide that it is, then you need to develop the paragraph in ways that will help the reader understand why this information is important.

Based on your experience as a reader of other people's writing, try to think of specific questions that your paragraph does not fully answer. Big, vague questions like "What does this mean?" will not give you the direction you need to make the paragraph fuller. Besides, such tough, sweeping questions imply a crabby sort of reader, with whom you will likely be defensive. Instead, imagine a curious reader, someone who really wants to hear what you have to say, someone you can teach about your subject. Begin your questions with words like "what," "how," and "why," which usually invite more than a "yes" or "no" answer.

Before attempting to rewrite your paragraph, take a few minutes to write down possible questions. Here is a sample of some reasonable questions that might be raised:

What exactly is a fantasy male? An illusion? Or someone's image of the ideal man?

How can I see these men more clearly? Is there any more information or description available about what they look like?

Why are the names interchangeable? Why is that important?

Even with this short list as a guide, you can begin rewriting with the intent of answering some of these specific questions more fully. You might want to freewrite some responses to particular questions first, or you might want to concentrate on just one or two questions as you begin revising. Here is an example of a rewritten paragraph that tries to answer the first two sets of questions with more explanation and more detail:

The male heroes of popular romance are pure formula figures designed to appeal to mainstream fantasies of the ideal man. Like the men photographed in women's fashion magazines, they share the same dominant physical features—

tall, dark, handsome, and white. For example, in the Harlequin Romance, *Ariana's Magic,* the hero, Marc Adams, is described in terms very similar to those used in the parody "Desire on Domino Island" to describe Rock Cliff. Both men are well built and muscular, with dark unruly hair, even features, and dark eyes. Both men have sensual mouths, a detail that signals the passionate love affair to come. Interestingly, both are described as world-weary, a suggestion that they are experienced men with pasts and problems and so, perhaps, in need of a loving female. In short, the male figure has an imposing, almost hypnotic, physical presence, which causes the heart of the heroine to beat rapidly. He may, for the sake of variation, be blond and blue-eyed, but he is always of a type—the all-American sex symbol as dictated by popular culture.

This revised paragraph has much more detail than the earlier version. By imagining what specifics your reader might need to know, you can more easily add the descriptions and explanations that flesh out your ideas. Suddenly, you are elaborating your ideas, rather than merely repeating or padding them.

Now you are ready to return to your list of reader's questions, and decide if you want to begin a new paragraph to deal with the concept of interchangeable names. The "why" question you have posed around this idea presents a different kind of challenge: the reader does not understand what you mean by interchangeable, nor, more significantly, grasp why this point is important to your argument. If you decide to keep this point, you will have to reconstruct the thinking process that generated it and spell out that thinking for your reader. Here is an example of how the concept might be explained and related more tightly to your essay's purpose:

The names given to the male heroes are extensions of the formula. Particular names do not signal individuality the way names often do in everyday life. If you were to ask a stranger to identify himself, he would usually give his name first as a way of distinguishing himself from others. The formula male, however, is not supposed to be distinguishable but recognizable. He is based on the notion of sameness, of repeating certain traits and features over and over. The name, therefore, is part of the packaging, often chosen for its sound or its masculine associations. Lee Smith chooses the name Rock Cliff to exaggerate this point—the name is hard sounding, and rough and tough. Even Marc Adams is a strong-sounding name. More importantly, it is a mainstream name with no hint of ethnicity. Finally, since all romance males are wealthy and successful, either artists or professionals, it is the kind of name that would look good on a letterhead or on the cover of a book. The names are interchangeable because the masculine traits and roles are interchangeable.

When you return to the list of questions after this revision, you may well decide that you now have provided enough detail to move on to other parts of your first draft. You may decide to leave some questions unanswered in favor of expanding your discussion of those you feel are most important to what you want to communicate. You may need to brainstorm or do a quick branching exercise to remind yourself of the thinking behind a particular point, or you may want to abandon an idea altogether and explore a new one. These are the kinds of decisions you make as a writer, but these decisions are easier when guided by the specific questions of a curious reader who can "talk" you through the process.

Write a Meta-Note

Metacognition means thinking about thinking, or being consciously aware of the processes of thinking. Accordingly, a *meta-note* is a note written to yourself, an instructor, or a writing partner that articulates the goals you wanted to achieve in the writing of an essay, and names some of the activities engaged in to achieve those goals.

As a revision strategy, writing a meta-note helps you focus on the overall structure and intent of a piece of writing, rather than merely on its word and sentence level. The strategy also emphasizes the point that writing is a form of communication. Generally, novice writers have difficulty recounting the kinds of decisions they have made during the composing process and why they have made them. Experienced writers, on the other hand, are better able to monitor their thinking and writing activities, to identify their goals, and to communicate those goals to their reader. Thus, writing a meta-note is a way of practicing your monitoring skills and of becoming more aware of the importance of having not only some goals when you are writing, but also some specific strategies for achieving those goals.

Illustration

The meta-note is most effective when it is written to and read by either your instructor or a writing partner who can give you some feedback. However, in the absence of a second person, you can still write the note to yourself in the role of reader and gain some useful insights into your own process of writing. The note should be very short—if you cannot articulate your major goals in a sentence or two, chances are you are not as clear about them as you ought to be. It follows, then, that the writing you have done will also not be as clear to your reader as it ought to be, and you will need to do some rethinking and rewriting. You should also use the meta-note to identify as specifically as you can what you did during the composing process to try to achieve your goals.

Here is a sample meta-note written after the final draft of an essay entitled "The Formula Male in Popular Romance":

Dear Reader,

My goal in this essay is to persuade you that popular romances are advertisements for falling in love—so the men in these books are merely part of the "sell" and completely stereotypical. To achieve my goal, I focus on four things—how the men look and their roles as rescuer, rake, and little boy. The formula of the romances is what sells them, and so men, and a particular sense of what is masculine, do not vary. I use two different books to make my case and draw many examples from the books to outline the formula as it applies to men.

This is a very clear and direct meta-note, suggesting that the writer has probably achieved the stated goals. There could be a little more awareness of process, but the writer can point to the division of material into four main areas, the importance of emphasizing the concept of "formula," and the use of examples and illustration. Although the writer of this meta-note probably will not revise the final draft on which it is based, the benefits of writing the meta-note can be applied to the next writing assignment. In other words, revision strategies can be developmental—crucial to the development of particular ideas, but also to the long-term development of writing and monitoring skills.

Now examine the following meta-note, based on the final draft of an essay that explores the diary of Anne Frank as an example of political testimony:

Dear Reader,

    My goal is to show that Anne Frank's diary and the
ending of the diary are against oppression. When I started,
I felt really good about this because it seemed original—I
mean using the diary is fine, but talking about how I felt
when the diary ended was the key. I had a lot of trouble
putting this feeling into words, and also there was so much
material to read about the deportations and the concen-
tration camps that I ran out of time. So I think the second
part of the essay has some problems, but I'm not sure how
to fix them.

To some extent, this meta-note is very sad: here is a writer who was
once excited by an idea and now sounds discouraged. But there is a
great deal of information in the meta-note that could help the writer
get back on track.

The first point is the shift away from the term "political testimony"
to the much more general phrase "against oppression." Since the writer
later complains about having too much information about the oppres-
sive conditions surrounding Anne Frank, it is likely that the composing process went awry here because of a loss of focus. If the goal were
restated to focus on the idea of political testimony, rather than on
oppression, the writer might see that much of the time-consuming
research on historical context might be unnecessary.

Most importantly, the meta-note also points to a precise place in the
composing process when the writer began to feel discouraged, so there
is an obvious starting place for revision. The writer might freewrite a
paragraph or two about the feelings inspired by the end of the diary,
or review what Allende has to say about political testimony, or do a
branching exercise around the concept of silence in an effort to rethink
or reconceptualize that part of the essay. The writer probably does not
know how to fix the problem because the common revision strategy of
word substitution is not likely to help here. What is required is a
reworking of the argument surrounding the diary's ending and the
concept of silence. Such a rethinking may renew the writer's sense of
excitement and save her from further blind alleys around the too vague
notion of oppression.

As you gain practice in writing meta-notes either to yourself or
another person, you will be improving your ability to think critically
about your writing, the specific goals you want to communicate, and
the strategies available to you—including more creative revisions than
those possible at the sentence or vocabulary level. After all, if an entire

section of an essay needs to be rewritten, there is little point tinkering with sentences that you may decide are no longer necessary. Remember that cosmetic changes to style and sentence structure should be held in reserve until you are satisfied that your major goals have been achieved. Meta-notes can help you decide what kind of revision you need to give priority to at a given point. Therefore, they can eliminate some of the frustration you may be experiencing.

Setting Up a Personalized Cycle of Revision

The knowledge that there are different cycles of revision, which are appropriate at different stages of the composing process, may in itself be enough to make revising a more rewarding experience. It is seldom necessary to start over completely; no matter how major the revision you decide to undertake, much of the work and thinking already done will not be wasted. For example, if the conclusion of your first draft makes clear that you have discovered new ideas while writing and perhaps changed the direction of an argument, you can go back and rewrite your introduction. Better still, you can use the conclusion of the first draft as the introduction to the second and so ensure that the new ideas are being set in an appropriate context. Students who decide to junk everything and choose a new topic are probably just stuck because they do not know when or what to revise.

In these cases, you may find it helpful to devise a revision checklist—one that not only reminds you of the different kinds of revision possible, but is also sensitive to your own needs as a writer. Basically, a personalized cycle of revision attempts to focus on different stages of composing and serves to remind you that revising is an ongoing process rather than just a final editing of your paper. If it is useful, cross-list the cycles with strategies that will help you gain more control over the writing and revising process.

Illustration

Your personalized cycle of revision can simply list activities that are part of the composing process, such as narrowing your subject or defining purpose. You can then use the list as a reminder of how these activities interrelate in such a way as to make revision natural. For example, generating ideas often leads to redefining purpose; drawing an issue tree to help you begin organizing often leads to a rethinking of the controlling statement. The sample cycle of revision given here uses a question format so that you can assess what you have written and what the appropriate level of attention for revision should be. The cycle also lists strategies that might be helpful.

Prewriting Revision Cycle

Is my subject specific and well defined?

Is the purpose explicit to my reader and appropriate to the course I am writing for?

What ideas must be included in my essay?

What ideas most interest me so far about my subject?

Have I explored a range of perspectives and thought about relationships among ideas?

Strategies: taking inventory, the observer's questions, the dictionary game, planning what and how, freewriting, branching.

Drafting Revision Cycle

What new ideas or directions emerged in the writing of the first draft?

Are my ideas well developed and is my thinking explained to the reader?

Does the current introduction give my reader the context my paper needs?

Is my controlling sentence clear and does it give my reader a sense of what to expect?

Have I ordered my material to support my goals in the most effective way?

Strategies: branching, developing a controlling statement, issue trees, freewriting an argumentative plan, talking to your reader, writing a meta-note.

Editing Revision Cycle

Is my word choice and tone appropriate for my reader and my subject?

Have I given the essay a title and properly documented the ideas of others?

Have I checked the final draft for errors in mechanics?

Sentence structure errors: pronoun references and
sentence fragments

Punctuation errors: comma splices

Spelling errors: words with *i* and *e*

Strategies: built-in time delay, reading aloud, reading to a writing partner.

As this personalized revision cycle makes clear, you should not focus on correcting and refining sentence structure and vocabulary until you have resolved all the larger concerns about content and organization. During editing, the cycle can be personalized to name specifically the kinds of errors you have made in the past and so might make again. Although your essay should be as free of mechanical errors as possible, it is important to emphasize that perfection is seldom, if ever, achievable. Even professional writers need editors who suggest clarification in style and catch occasional slips in grammar. By personalizing the categories of sentence structure, punctuation, and spelling, you can train yourself to look for the errors that you tend to make, rather than trying to read for all possible errors.

The strategies for editing are limited. You can read your paper aloud and mark any sentences that sound odd or require more than one reading. Very likely, these sentences will need revision. If you are lucky enough to have a writing partner, you can ask him or her to circle unclear words or terms and point out grammatical errors. A good, basic text on grammar, together with a dictionary and a thesaurus, should be part of every college student's survival kit. If you decide to keep raiding the thesaurus as a revision strategy, remember to double-check word substitutions in the dictionary to make sure that the new word fits the context of your sentence.

Reading what you are writing and have written is crucial to generating, connecting, and communicating ideas. The key to effective revision is to read for different purposes at different times in the composing process: to read for yourself to generate ideas; to read for content and design of argument; and to read with the eyes of your reader to determine what questions need a fuller answer. Being aware of the cycles of revision is also crucial. Frequent searches for just the right word in the early stages of composing interrupt and may completely halt the flow of your ideas. Nor will just one desperate rereading at the end help you to improve your essay. But if you can appreciate that there are different cycles of revision, you may find the editing cycle becoming less painful. Most importantly, you will have strategies that are more creative and certainly less frustrating than the scratch-out-and-start-over approach.

WRITING JOURNALS AND WRITING PARTNERS

Keeping a writing journal between essay assignments and working with a partner during the writing of assignments are two long-term strategies that can dramatically improve your skills as a critical writer. Both are effective because they require an active commitment—you learn by doing, by practicing, and by interacting with another writer. Although both strategies require a considerable investment of time and effort, they are more successful than any single strategy in helping you become more conscious of how you write and how you can gain more control over the writing process. In a sense, these are "umbrella" strategies under which more specific strategies can be gathered and applied.

If you decide to keep a writing journal or to work with a writing partner—or to do both—you must be willing to stand by your commitment for at least one academic term, and preferably longer, in order to reap the greatest benefit. Because writing is a complex task, a sustained and deliberate effort to improve your writing over time is a much safer bet than the lure of the quick fix. Moreover, these strategies involve a variety of tasks and so are seldom boring; and they can radically change how you feel about writing by helping you build your confidence.

This section offers some guidelines as to how to get started, but feel free to experiment as you go along. You might also ask your writing instructor for advice, or, if your college has a writing lab or center, you could talk over your plans with one of the instructors there. It is important to think carefully about what you want to do, and what you can expect; otherwise, it will be difficult for you to devote the necessary time. You should enjoy these strategies, and increasing the amount of pleasure you experience around writing is not an unreasonable goal.

Writing Journals

If you decide to keep a journal, you should write in it four or five days a week, for fifteen minutes or so. Some experts claim that simply doing this for five, ten, or fifteen weeks—always the longer the better—

will make you a better writer than you are now.[3] The key is to write for yourself and to write freely, without the pressures of deadlines and grades and without pausing for editing at the sentence and word level. Write often, and write as much as you can.

Obviously, you should feel free to write about whatever stirs your curiosity, interest, anger, imagination, and so on. However, if you write about writing, you can also keep a log of your progress as a writer, a kind of verbal chart of what you do when you write, your blind alleys and brick walls, as well as your breakthroughs. It is a good idea to date your entries, so that, as you reread what you have written, you can assess your own development and insights. Here are suggestions of topics you can write about:

The rules you learned about essay writing in high school

How you felt about your last essay—during and after the writing

A summary of the feedback you usually receive from instructors

A description of how you think instructors grade essays

A quick response to something you have read, or to a lecture or class discussion

A risky but intriguing idea for an essay

A strong opinion you hold about something

A summary of a particular strategy you applied to help you generate ideas

An examination of the part of essay writing you like or like the least

Meta-notes to yourself or to your writing partner

A reexamination or a rethinking of an earlier journal entry

A letter to an author whose work you have been reading

As you can see from this list of suggestions, it is a good idea to vary both the tasks and the tone of your writing. You should be silly, as well as serious. You should write about what frustrates you, but also about what is working, what feels good when you are composing. The more you write, the more insights and critical awareness you will gain about how you write and how to solve writing problems. If you are uncertain what to write about on a given day, you can use your journal as a kind

3. Dana C. Elder, *Writing to Write* (New York: Macmillan, 1990) 18–19.

of playing ground for trying out some of the strategies explained in this handbook.

Finally, you should decide how private or public you want your journal to be. You may feel that privacy gives you the safety net you need to take some risks in your thinking and to be totally honest about your opinions and your progress. Or you may want an instructor or a writing partner to look at some of what you write in order to give you some feedback. If you are working with a partner, there are some points to consider that will guide your interactions.

Writing Partners

Having a writing partner or being a member of a small group that meets regularly to discuss writing yields a number of benefits. First, and most obviously, your partner can provide the fresh eyes or the more distanced perspective, which you naturally lose when grappling with an essay topic or writing problem. In other words, your partner can be your first reader, asking questions to help you expand your ideas and pointing out any gaps in communication.

Writing partners, however, are important to the entire process of composing, not just to the cycles of revision. Many people find it desirable to talk out an idea before attempting a first draft. Therefore, carrying on a dialogue with a writing partner, whose questions often lead to a clearer sense of purpose and argument, can prove to be vital to prewriting. More than a word or sentence editor, your partner is an intelligent listener and questioner who can help you discover a subject, analyze an assignment, or suggest a strategy that might solve a particular writing problem. It is often a revelation for novice writers to learn that experienced writers talk over their ideas and seek this kind of advice about writing on a regular basis. This is particularly true for essay writing, in which imagining an audience and persuading that audience is an essential part of communicating. Whereas novice writers tend to feel shy and overly protective about their ideas, experienced writers often use exploratory conversations to help them articulate their ideas and their goals.

Besides knowing that you should be able to consult your writing partner throughout the composing process, you also need to think about the reciprocity of such partnerships. As partner to another writer, you, too, will be expected to listen, question, suggest strategies, and evaluate someone else's drafts. Though most people tend to think first about how a writing partner might help them, the act of helping in return is probably the most significant factor in the long-term success of this strategy. Recent studies of peer tutoring and student evaluation suggest that there are considerable gains in all aspects of writing when students read each other's writing and try to teach each other how to write more effectively.[4]

You may choose to form a writing partnership with just one person or with two or three people. It is easier to schedule meetings with one person, but working with a small group tends to ensure a variety of perspectives and approaches to writing problems. You might want to begin working with one person and then gradually expand the group once you have learned some guidelines for effective interaction. Most experts agree that you should choose as your writing partner, someone you do not know, for then writing, not a previous friendship, becomes the reason for meeting, and advice and suggestions can sometimes be exchanged more freely. However, if it is too difficult or awkward to set up a partnership this way, working with a friend is preferable to not acting on this strategy at all. Perhaps the best solution is for two sets of friends to form a group of four and so take advantage of both established trust and the need to meet and interact with writing as the central focus. Once a group has been formed, it is crucial that all parties agree to a workable set of guidelines. In addition to the suggestions given here, you might want to consult a writing instructor at your college to help you get started.

Guidelines for Writing Partners

1. Partners or group members should meet regularly, in between essay assignments, as well as during the writing of essays.
2. Partners are not coauthors—the goal is not to tell a partner what to do or to change a partner's argument, but to make observations and suggestions as a reader.
3. Mix your comments—a partner should point out what is good and effective, as well as what might be improved.
4. Ask questions that are specific rather than broad. A comment like "I don't get your main point" is not nearly as helpful as "Here is where you lose me—how do you get from A to B?"
5. Try to limit editorial suggestions to two or three—too many comments can overwhelm a writer.

4. Mary H. Beaven, "Individualized Goal Setting, Self-Evaluation, and Peer Evaluation," *Evaluating Writing,* ed. Charles R. Cooper and Lee Odell (Urbana, IL: National Council of Teachers of English, 1977) 135–53.

6. As a writer, try to accept criticism without being defensive—your partner is a kind of safety net, so use the partnership (or group) for taking risks, asking questions no matter how trivial they may seem, and making mistakes.

Of course, the actual dynamics of a partnership or writing group are more complex than this short list of guidelines implies. You will have to work out your own style of interaction and be patient enough to build trust, while establishing a fair exchange of information and workload. The key is to start, to try a few meetings, and perhaps meet with an expert on writing if problems occur that neither partner can solve.

Over time, your writing partner (or group) will actually become a learning partner, a catalyst for all kinds of critical thinking activities and active exchange of ideas. People do not have to think and write in isolation in order to be independent thinkers and writers. It is only by exchanging ideas and information that you learn how to listen to others, how to evaluate their ideas, and how to recognize what is special about your own.

ACKNOWLEDGMENTS

(continued from p. iv)

Part 1

© 1988 by Temple University. Reprinted by permission of Temple University Press.

Far Side copyright 1993 FARWORKS, INC./Dist. by Universal Press Syndicate. Reprinted with permission. All rights reserved.

William Grossman. MODERN BRAZILIAN SHORT STORIES, 'Metonymy, or the Husband's Revenge' pages 27–32. Used with permission.

Part 2

Copr. © 1940 James Thurber. Copr. © 1968 Helen Thurber. From *Fables For Our Time*, published by Harper Collins.

Townsend, John Rowe, from New Community, Summer 1976. Used by permission of John Rowe Townsend.

The BIZARRO cartoon by Dan Piraro is reprinted by permission of Chronicle Books, San Francisco, CA.

Batcher, Elaine. "'Nothing Special:' The Portrayal of Girls and Women in Current Junior Grade Readers." *Canadian Woman Studies*, Spring 1987, Volume 8, #1, pp. 35–37. This article was based on 1975 and 1986 research projects to evaluate school texts commissioned by the Federation of Women Teachers' Associations of Ontario, authored by Elaine Batcher, researcher and writer of education theory; Alison Winter, teacher with the Halton Board of Education in Ontario; and Vicki Wright, past president of the North York Women Teachers' Association of Ontario. All three have taught elementary school.

INDEX

patterns of words and images in, 44
text of, 22–32
title of, 46–47

Haas, Christina, 20
Hill, Carol, 93
Holmberg, Carol, 110
Holst, Spencer, 101–103, 110–112
How plans, 128
Humor
lateral thinking and, 129
as persuasive technique, 108, 109
Hunches, 96–97

Idea generation
branching as method of, 129–130, 140–142
dictionary game as method of, 144–146
observer's questions as method of, 142–144
Images
reading for patterns of, 44–46
to express gender, 32–33, 149–150
Instincts, 96–97
Intentional fallacy, 109
Inventories, 124–126
Issue trees, 154–155

Journals
guidelines for, 48–49
writing, 170–172

Komunyakaa, Yusef, 142, 143

Language
bias in, 69–70
development of sensitivity to, 35–38
emotive, 70
euphemistic, 70–71
used for advertising, 71
Larson, Gary, 158
Lateral thinking
explanation of, 62, 129
generation of ideas as, 129
positive and negative comparison questions as, 104–105
role-playing as example of, 94
to solve open-ended problems, 64–66
vertical vs., 62–63
"why" technique as tool of, 79
Logic puzzles, 63–64

Maps
construction of mental, 50–51
developing framework for critical thinking as method of, 106
illustration of mental, 51–53
what and how plans as, 127
Masculinity
images in popular romance novels of, 149–150, 161–163
images used to express, 32–33
words linked to, 44
Mental maps
construction of, 50–51
illustration of, 51–53
Metacognition, 164
Meta-notes
benefits of, 166–167
examples of, 165, 166
explanation of, 164
writing, 164–165
Metaphor, 36–37